TWENTIETH CENTURY PEOPLE

MONTGOMERY OF ALAMEIN

THE GENERAL WHO NEVER LOST A CAMPAIGN

TWENTIETH CENTURY PEOPLE

MONTGOMERY OF ALAMEIN

THE GENERAL WHO NEVER LOST A CAMPAIGN

BY JOHN O. H. FISHER

HODDER AND STOUGHTON
LONDON SYDNEY AUCKLAND TORONTO

British Library Cataloguing in Publication Data
Fisher, John O. H.
    Montgomery of Alamein. – (Twentieth century
    people; 4).
    1. Montgomery, Bernard Law, *Viscount Montgomery*
    – Juvenile literature
    2. Great Britain. Army – Biography –
    Juvenile literature
    3. Generals – Great Britain – Biography –
    Juvenile literature
    I. Series
    355.3'32'0924   DA69.3.M56

    ISBN 0-340-25558-7

Text copyright © 1981 John O. H. Fisher
First published 1981.

Printed in Great Britain for Hodder and Stoughton Children's
Books, a division of Hodder and Stoughton Ltd, Mill Road,
Dunton Green, Sevenoaks, Kent TN13 2YJ by
Morrison & Gibb Ltd, London and Edinburgh.
Photoset by Rowland Phototypesetting Ltd, Bury St Edmunds, Suffolk.

Contents

1
A Rebel in Tasmania

What do you think makes a good general? Is it how many battles he wins? Or the gains that result from them? Or the difficulties he overcomes? Or the planning which enables the battles to be won? Or is it the qualities of leadership?

Judged by any of these tests, Bernard Montgomery, super-commander of Britain's armies in the decisive battles of World War II, deserves a high rating. Certainly his victory at El Alamein changed the course of the War in Egypt, just as his triumph at Falaise in Normandy broke the German armies on the western front. He was feared and admired as a commander by the Germans and respected by the Russians.

He was unusual as a person, as well as a general. He was short. His face was gaunt and rather fox-like. His eyes, light blue-grey, were so deeply set that you sometimes got the impression that they were watching you intently from behind a mask.

He was cocksure, tactless, impatient, domineering, and a bit of a showman. He was also uncompromising: in his view, there were only two possible solutions to any military problem – his own, and the wrong one. He was so competitive that he became unpopular with many of his fellow officers, with the War Office, and, later, with his American allies.

Yet he had a sense of humour and a knowledge of human nature. Few, if any, generals have been as successful in keeping in touch with the men under their command. The average soldier had never known a general who took so much trouble to interest and inspire him. Whether in training exercises or on the eve of battle, he would call on unit after unit, telling each group to gather round and listen, taking them into his confidence, explaining clearly and simply how he intended to carry out his plans. The men soon learnt, too, that when Montgomery said they would have supplies and ammunition, they could rely on getting them. Their spirits rose whenever they saw him.

True success did not come to Montgomery until he was 54. 'Make your big effort early on in life,' he once told a schoolboy. 'I nearly left mine too late.' But when it came, success was meteoric. Up till the summer of 1942, almost no one outside the Army had heard of Montgomery. Then suddenly, that autumn, the great leader appeared. Some people supposed that only Army red tape had prevented this brilliant man from bounding to the top years earlier.

But his family were as surprised as the general public to learn that they had a top-rank military leader among them. They had known Bernard a long time, and never considered him to be a genius.

*   *   *

It all began one day in September 1889 when a small steamer, the *S.S. Tainui*, equipped with four old-fashioned masts and a single funnel, sailed from London bound for Australia.

Bernard Montgomery, not yet two years old, was one of the passengers. His father, Henry Montgomery, had recently been consecrated Bishop of Tasmania, the island lying off Australia's southern coast – and the new Bishop was taking his wife and family with him.

When the job was first offered to him, Henry Montgomery was not very sure where to find Tasmania on the map. But he accepted the challenge even before looking at an atlas. He had not consulted his wife either – partly because she was one of those Victorian wives who left the big decisions to their husbands, and partly because, in an age when seniority counted, she was almost a generation younger than her husband.

Theirs was a strange romance, for Maud Farrar

The Montgomery family at home at New Park, Ireland, in 1886, before Bernard was born. His mother is sitting on the bench with two children, while his father stands behind, holding Harold. On their left are Henry Montgomery's parents. (Col. Brian Montgomery)

was only 11 and Henry Montgomery 29 years old, when they first met. She was one of five good-looking daughters of Dr Farrar, Dean of Westminster, for whom Henry Montgomery had worked as curate.

Dr Farrar was a fashionable and controversial preacher. He was so successful in arousing a sense of sin among his listeners that, when he was known to be speaking in Westminster Abbey, they often had to put up notices outside reading ABBEY FULL to keep away the late-comers. Dr Farrar also wrote best-selling books of moral improvement and instruction, one of which *Eric or Little by Little* chronicled the fate of a schoolboy whose downfall began from the moment when he indulged in the mildest of swear-words. Dr Farrar, horrified by the drunkenness that prevailed in the back streets of Westminster, had also taken the pledge never to touch a drop of alcohol. He did not smoke, either.

These were high standards even for those days. Yet it was clear that, in the eyes of Dr Farrar, Henry Montgomery fully lived up to them. For the Dean allowed his daughter to become engaged to Henry while she was still 14 – provided that she did not breathe a word about it, even to her sisters.

She wore no engagement ring and, up to within a few days of her wedding, was still doing lessons in the schoolroom. There were no years of independence for her, and no opportunities for her to make any other choice. She was married in Westminster Abbey on July 28th, 1881, still not 17 years old.

Then came children – nine in all. First Sybil (nicknamed Queenie) in 1882, Harold in 1883 and Donald in 1886. Bernard, the future Field Marshal, was born on November 17th, 1887, and Una shortly before the family left for Tasmania. That made five, and there were four more to come – Desmond, Winsome, Brian and Colin.

*   *   *

The Montgomery family arrived in the harbour of Hobart, the capital of Tasmania, in October 1889, and the new Bishop learnt that his diocese was not only nearly as large as Scotland, but twice as difficult to get round. There were no railways on the island, and, once outside Hobart, few passable roads. Steep mountain ranges and deep ravines divided the country. Goods had to be carried on pack-horses, sometimes along paths that fell so sharply that riders thought it safer to dismount.

When the Bishop went on tour, he took tents with him and ate bacon, hardbake biscuit, and cocoa cooked in a billycan. His flock included ex-convicts, whalers, gold miners and aborigines. He even visited the lighthouses sprinkled along Tasmania's rocky coast. Sometimes, he would have to be away from home for more than six months of the year.

But Maud Montgomery could be relied on to keep up the standards without his help. With her dark hair, violet eyes and cream complexion, she was something of a beauty, and many of those who knew that the Montgomery family came from Donegal took her for an Irish colleen, although her ancestry was British. She was a dashing horsewoman, and looked the part in her well-cut blue riding habit. She could drive a dogcart (a small carriage seating one couple facing forwards and another facing aft) with skill and confidence. She could even manage horses harnessed in tandem one in front of the other, and would sometimes startle holiday-makers by riding at breakneck speed along the shore – side-saddle, of course.

Maud allowed her family to mix with Tasmanians – particularly the children of clergy, schoolmasters or parish workers. But one thing she would not permit. No child of hers was to pick up a Tasmanian accent; and when any of the family 'talked Tasmanian' even in fun, there was trouble. The sinner was made to repeat the word in standard English.

At times the Montgomerys dressed in style, and the family on its way to the Cathedral was a sight to behold, the Bishop with his patriarchal beard, Mrs Montgomery in black satin, the boys in red berets, black breeches and short covert coats and the girls in dresses of a kind now only to be seen in Victorian picture-books.

But keeping up appearances was not always easy. There was a slump on the Australian mainland during the early 1890s. Several banks failed, including one in Tasmania. For a time the family had to do without a carriage, or even horses, and they could not afford a gardener. In a year when the Bishop felt obliged to contribute £300 to the rebuilding of the Cathedral chancel, Maud took pride in being the worst-dressed woman in Hobart. It could hardly have improved her temper. The Montgomerys survived only through selling off a part of the family estate in Ireland.

Their home in Tasmania, known as Bishopscourt, was well suited to the needs of a large family. It was a rambling house with views over the harbour on one side and of Mount Wellington on the other.

Bishopscourt, Hobart, the family home in Tasmania. (Col. Brian Montgomery)

One room had been adapted for use as a chapel, and another had been built on outside the house as a classroom. For Maud had seen to it that tutors came out from England to watch over the family's education.

A home of this kind, with nine children in it, could not be run without discipline, and Maud Montgomery insisted that her sons and daughters conformed to it. Even the Bishop went to his wife before he went on tour to draw the 'pocket money' he would need for small extras. The children got up at daybreak and tidied their rooms, made their own beds and cleaned their own shoes. The boys chopped the firewood. Lessons began at half past seven, after which, there was room-inspection, with each child standing, on parade, in his or her doorway. Then prayers, and only after that breakfast.

In the evening, the boys cooked their own supper and took it in turn to choose and buy the food. They ate the meal in the schoolroom.

13

Sunday meant not only Morning Prayer but learning the Collect, reading aloud from the Bible, and no games or friends to tea. No sweets were allowed because it was thought they accounted for the bad teeth which many Australians then had. Smoking, of course, was also forbidden and bad manners severely punished with the culprit being sent off to bed – even in the midst of a party. Or Maud might choose to beat him. She also gave a beating to any child that misused its pocket money.

Bernard, somehow, seemed to get into more scrapes than any of the other children. He not only spent some of his pocket money on sweets, he publicly defied his mother by accepting them when they were offered at friends' houses. At one point, he became an enthusiastic stamp collector and sold his bicycle in order to buy some stamps he particularly wanted. His mother disapproved, because the bicycle had been a present and therefore must not be parted with. She bought it back, and stopped all Bernard's pocket money until he had repaid her every penny.

He had a mischievous streak and could never resist a temptation to encourage his brothers and sisters to perform feats of daring – such as climbing from one first floor window of the house to the next by linking hands or swinging down to the ground through the outer branches of the trees, monkey fashion. Hide and seek on the roof of the house was one of his favourite games.

He suffered for his independence. On one memorable day he was caught smoking. His father took him into the Montgomery private chapel and the two spent a quarter of an hour in silent prayer,

14

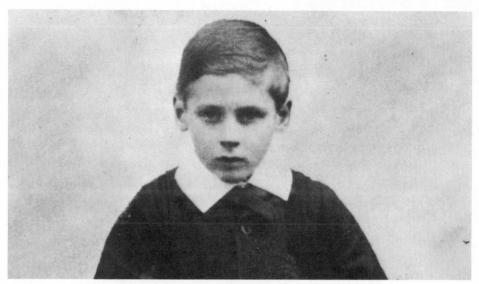

Bernard, aged 10. (Col. Brian Montgomery)

at the end of which the Bishop was able to assure his
son that God would overlook his sin because he had
confessed it. But Bernard's mother was less for-
giving than God, and was waiting outside the chapel
door to punish her son in her own less spiritual style.

He probably caused her more trouble than any of
her other children. Harold and Donald, the two elder
boys, were placid and obedient. They kept each other
occupied, and were not willing to join in Bernard's
escapades. The younger children were more easily
managed and gave little trouble. That left Bernard
out on his own.

It was a clash of wills between mother and son to
show who was the stronger, and his mother sometimes punished Bernard without even telling him
what he had done wrong. The result could have been
foreseen. The more ill-used and unloved Bernard felt
himself to be, the more anxious he was to draw his
mother's attention to himself – even if that meant
misbehaving. And the more he was punished for

15

misbehaving, the more of an outcast he felt. Things went from bad to worse.

But there were many happy days too. One of the never-to-be-broken rules of the house was that there was to be peace and quiet during the period between lunch and tea, when Maud Montgomery liked to have her afternoon nap. No one, except the Bishop, who, if at home, would be working quietly in his study, was allowed in the house. The rest of the family could do what they liked or go where they liked as long as they could not be heard. This was the best time to go riding, or swimming or fishing or on picnics.

Nevertheless, the feeling remained with Bernard that he had been unfairly treated and he never fully forgave his mother. 'One was hemmed in . . . one was opposed,' he would say, speaking of his childhood. 'One had to break out.'

*　　*　　*

The break-out, when it happened, did not take place in Tasmania, but afterwards, and then only as a result of a chain of quite unforeseen events.

The nearby Bishopric of Melanesia, covering islands in the South Pacific, became vacant, and Bishop Montgomery was asked to take temporary control. His work there among the natives was so successful that he was asked, in a cable signed by both the Archbishop of Canterbury and the Archbishop of York, to resign his own bishopric and return to London to take over and run the Society for the Propagation of the Gospel.

It was a blow for the Montgomerys, who were now

16

looking forward to spending their lives in Tasmania.

But, once again, the Bishop's sense of duty triumphed, and by Christmas 1901 the family was back in England.

They settled into a large house in Bolton Road, Chiswick, near the River Thames, not far from the finishing post of the Oxford and Cambridge Boat Race. Harold had decided to emigrate to South Africa, but Donald and Bernard were both sent as day boys to St Paul's School, which at that time was near the Olympia Exhibition Hall.

The School had been founded in the time of Henry VIII by John Colet, Dean of St Paul's, and had been chosen by the Montgomerys partly because of its connection with the Church and for its academic reputation, but also because only a day school would allow Maud Montgomery to see her boys every morning and every evening, and so, as she thought, retain her control of them. She probably hoped that one of them would become a clergyman.

She had, however, misjudged the affair, for one of the features of St Paul's was its Army Class, in which the timetable and subjects taught were specially designed to suit those boys who had de-cided to choose the Army as their career. And on his very first day at school, Bernard, along with the other new boys, was asked if he wished to join the Army Class. His hand was one of the first to be raised.

It seems doubtful whether he had ever thought before of becoming a soldier, but here at last was a chance to make an important decision entirely on his own. And he took it. There was no more talk of his going into the Church.

17

2

 A Cadet out
of Step

Montgomery was already 19 years old in 1906 when he left St Paul's School, and a master at that time described him as 'rather backward for his age'. But this was not altogether surprising. Up to the age of 14 he had never been to school. All that he had learned came to him from tutors sent out from England, and they had evidently taught him very little. There was also the fact that he was a 'colonial' and therefore somewhat looked down on.

Montgomery himself said that when he came to England he had little learning and no culture. He had not played either cricket or football – the games which really counted at an English public school. But he was very fit and a powerful swimmer and he found it easy to build on these assets. In little more than three years he became captain of the school Rugby XV and was picked for the Cricket First XI. He also earned a reputation for tough tackling on the football field.

Here was success. Here were people he could lead and organise. But unfortunately this kind of advancement was no help to him in his ambition to make a career for himself in the Army, and, after three years, the masters who taught him were none too hopeful about his prospects. 'To have a serious chance for Sandhurst (the next step forward in a

Bernard setting out from the house in Chiswick to cycle to school at St. Paul's, about 1904. (Col. Brian Montgomery)

career), he must give more time for work,' one report said. The warning came as a shock to Montgomery. It brought him up short – and from then on he paid more attention to what went on in the classroom.

In fact, young Bernard not only passed the competitive examination to Sandhurst without any extra cramming but was placed more than halfway up the list – 72nd out of some 170 candidates who were accepted as cadets.

Montgomery himself admitted, however, that the standards were not overwhelmingly high. In those days the Army did not attract the best brains. It was a profession which appealed first and foremost to those whose fathers, and perhaps grandfathers, had served in the Army. Others were drawn to it by the

kind of life led by officers in peacetime: travel, and
service abroad, with plenty of time in between for
hunting, polo, and regimental dinners and balls.
Sometimes it was the profession into which families
put their younger sons, for whom no other suitable
employment could be found in politics, a learned
profession, or the family estate.

But, from the start, for the career of officer and
gentlemen one needed money. The sons of officers
who had served in the Army were taken at Sandhurst at reduced fees, but the son of a civilian had to
pay £150 to cover board and lodging during the
term-time and, although this was supposed to cover
all expenses, some pocket money was needed. After
some discussion, in which Bernard's mother would
undoubtedly have played a large part, he was
allowed the sum of £2 a month, which was to
continue during the holidays – giving him a total of
£24 a year. It was not enough to buy him a wrist-
watch, which all the other cadets seemed to have.

*   *   *

But the special problems of one new cadet would not
have greatly worried the officers in charge of the
Royal Military College at Sandhurst in the far-off
days of January, 1907.

Indeed the Army had barely confronted the reali-
ties of the new century.

Britain had fought no major war since the
Crimean War more than fifty years – say two
generations – earlier. The conflicts in which the
Army had since been engaged were mainly against

upstart tribes in far-off lands, which could easily be subdued. The main exception to this was the Boer war, fought in South Africa to retain control of the Transvaal's gold and diamond mines, and in this there had been a number of costly defeats, which had exposed weaknesses not only in the Army's methods of warfare, but in its intelligence and communications systems.

But all this was a matter for the General Staff of the War Office in Whitehall in London, and they were not only remote but were also highly unpopular at Sandhurst.

And even the General Staff were not able to do a great deal to modernise the Army. As the government of the day saw it, it was the Navy that should get the lion's share of the money available for defence. It was the Royal Navy, often described as the Senior Service, which protected the vital trade routes of the British Empire. And as the German navy began to increase in fire-power and numbers, more and more money was needed for the British Admiralty to keep pace. 'The British Army,' as one admiral put it, 'is merely a projectile fired by the Royal Navy.'

Down at Sandhurst, the horse was still supreme, and those who could ride well were well-placed for promotion. Moreover, cross-country riding – including fox-hunting – was considered to give officers 'an eye for the country', that is the knack of deciding correctly which are the strong or weak points in your own – or an enemy's – front, and which are the most promising lines of advance and communication.

Machine guns were all very well in their way, but

their usefulness depended on the speed with which replacement ammunition could be brought to them, which, in the days before mechanical transport, was a limiting factor.

The subjects taught at Sandhurst were, though useful, fairly elementary. They included mathematics, the laws of war, map-reading, engineering, administration, tactics, drill, gymnastics, riding and fencing.

The cadets were judged partly on their proficiency in these subjects but also on their willingness to learn, their attitude towards the officers who supervised their instruction, their relations with fellow cadets, and on whether they fitted in to the Army's life-style. Assessed by these standards, Montgomery's score was not likely to be a high one.

He did not look the officer type. He was not a 'fine figure of a man' but short-statured, and by no means handsome. His features were narrow – almost pinched. He was not forthcoming; he did not smile readily. He did not take for granted everything he was told, and he did not believe that prowess in the hunting field was an aid to victory on the field of battle.

His resources did not allow him to join in the amusements of his fellow cadets – shooting parties, for instance, or expeditions to London. Nor was he dazzled by the splendour of regimental uniforms or the spit and polish which officers were supposed to encourage for its own sake among their men.

He was just not interested in girls – which was probably just as well on his income. When he got leave he preferred to spend it with the family in Ireland, playing hide and seek in the rambling

Above: *The Sandhurst Rugby XV, 1908.*
Centre: *Cadets building a bridge.* (National Army Museum)
Left: *Bernard as a cadet at Sandhurst.* (Col. Brian Montgomery)

family house, eating vast teas of Irish potato scones and soda bread, fishing for conger eels and mackerel from an open sailing boat.

But at first things went extremely well. Montgomery was very soon picked for the Royal Military College Rugby XV and helped the team to inflict a severe defeat on its great rival, the Woolwich Royal Military Academy. After six weeks, he was promoted to Lance-Corporal – usually a sign of further advancement to come.

But for Bernard, his promotion to Lance-Corporal was partly the reason why he got into trouble – for instead of sobering him down, it made him more overbearing and reckless as the leader of the junior section of 'B' Company. And the reason was that Sandhurst was, in some ways, rather like a public school of the type that Montgomery himself and most of the other cadets had only recently left. That is, the senior officers relied to some extent on the cadets themselves to knock each other into shape and to discipline any who stepped out of line.

There was a good deal of practical joking, too. This seems to have been a traditional sport at Sandhurst.

Certainly in Montgomery's time there was permanent warfare between the cadets of 'A' Company and those of Company 'B', who lived on the floor below. The battles were fought with war cries and forays, often led by Montgomery. But one day he went too far.

Descending with a band of followers shortly before the dinner hour, he found an unlucky victim in the midst of changing into evening clothes – about to put on his trousers. Montgomery ordered him to be held at bayonet point and his arms pinioned behind his back. Then he was blindfolded and his shirt tails were set on fire. The cadet was badly burnt and had to go to the military hospital, and, though he refused to say who had done the deed, it was traced to Montgomery.

Understandably, the Commandant took the view that this was something more serious than a practical joke. It showed a lack of judgment – and irresponsibility. It raised the question of whether Montgomery had the right qualities to make a good officer. Did his lack of consideration for others make him unfit to command a body of men?

For a time it was uncertain whether Bernard would be allowed to stay on. His mother came down to Sandhurst to see the Commandant in the hope of avoiding the disgrace that would descend on the Bishop if it became known that his son had been forced to leave Sandhurst for riotous misconduct.

In the end the Commandant decided to reduce Bernard to the ranks at once, which meant that instead of passing out of Sandhurst at the end of a year, he would have to stay a further six months.

*   *   *

It was a set-back both to Bernard and his family. But, once again, shock treatment worked, and Bernard started to make up lost ground. His principal aim, now, was to do well enough in his passing out examinations to be selected for the Indian Army.

His reasoning was simple. Under the circumstances of the time, he simply could not afford to join one of the home regiments. If he did so, he would be paid five shillings and threepence (26p) a day as a Second Lieutenant or six shillings and sixpence (32½p) when promoted to Lieutenant. But his mess bill (the cost of food etc. eaten with the other officers) would alone come to more than his total pay, and it was generally reckoned that, even in an unfashionable regiment, a private income of at least £100 a year was needed. Bernard did not wish to call on his parents for more help than they had already given.

In the Indian Army he could live on his pay from the start. But the trouble was that the Indian Army normally accepted only the top 30 of the candidates in the Sandhurst passing-out examination. Very occasionally, the number was stretched to 35. Unluckily, Bernard's placing in the pass-out examination was 36th.

It was a bitter blow; however all was not lost. Bernard's marks were good enough to make it almost certain that the regiment he picked as his second choice would accept him.

After making enquiries, he applied to join the Royal Warwickshire Regiment. The Regiment was a well established one – originally raised back in 1674 for service under William of Orange. Yet it was not fashionable or expensive. Best of all, one of its two regular battalions was in India.

And so, with two other ex-Sandhurst men, he joined the Royal Warwickshires and found himself one cold evening in December 1908 in the ante-room of the Officers' Mess at Peshawar on the North-West Frontier of India, at that time still ruled from London under a Viceroy.

There was one other officer in the ante-room. He at once said, 'Have a drink', and rang for the waiter.

Montgomery was not thirsty. But two whiskies arrived and he had to drink one of them. It was the first time in his life that he had drunk alcohol. And that was only the beginning. All the newly joined officers of the Regiment had to call on the other units of the Regiment and leave cards at the Officers' Messes. At each he was offered a drink – and it was considered bad form to ask for an orange squash or lemonade. 'I have always disliked alcohol since then,' Montgomery afterwards wrote.

He learned to dislike formal regimental dinners, too. Indeed, the climate and the habits of those who served in India were enough to undermine the strongest constitution after more than a few years, and Montgomery eventually came to be glad that he hadn't passed out higher from Sandhurst for permanent service in India.

Scene on the North-West Frontier (the Khyber Pass). Montgomery became quite an expert on mules. (BBC Hulton)

He never became interested in the art of the country, its customs or its history. What absorbed him was the Army and its organisation. He was appointed Assistant Adjutant (the Adjutant is the officer who helps to arrange the duties of military units allotted to him) and later Regimental Quartermaster responsible for maintaining supplies of food, ammunition and other stores.

He was also Officer in charge of Regimental Games. He was enthusiastic enough to learn two of the local languages – Urdu and Pushtu. He even became something of an expert on mules and mule transport on which the regiment depended.

In 1913, the battalion returned to England, with Montgomery as enthralled as ever by the Army.

At 26 he was still a Lieutenant, with the feeling that something, he wasn't quite sure what, was wrong with the Army, yet uncertain of what to study and how to find out what needed putting right.

The First World War of 1914–1918 was to give him some of the answers.

3
 Distinguished
Service

War between Britain and Germany was declared on
August 4th, 1914 with Britain and France as allies.
The struggle afterwards became known as World
War I, though Montgomery preferred to call it the
Kaiser's War. A British Expeditionary Force was
assembled in the United Kingdom with all possible
speed to help the French armies on the continent of
Europe.

Montgomery was playing tennis at Folkestone
when the order came to mobilise for action. Like
other officers, he had no idea of what was going to
happen. But his Commanding Officer had some
advice for him: 'The shorter your hair is when on a
campaign, the easier it is to keep it clean.' Montgomery wondered if he should take some money
with him when he went overseas. And the C.O. re-
assured him on this point as well. 'Money would be
useless on a campaign', he said. 'Everything that is
needed will be provided.' Montgomery rejected both
these recommendations. He had his hair cut
'decently short' as usual, by a civilian barber in
Folkestone, and drew out £10 in sovereigns and
half-sovereigns from the bank.

On the third day of the mobilisation, officers had
to take their swords to the regimental armourer to
have them sharpened for battle – which mystified

Montgomery, who had never been told how to use one except on ceremonial parades.

On August 23rd, nineteen days after the war had begun, Montgomery's regiment reached Boulogne.

Three days later, after a night march, he and his battalion arrived at the village of Haucourt, not far south of the Belgian border.

The idea was to hold off a German thrust southwards through Belgium. At Haucourt, another battalion from Montgomery's Division was further ahead, and he could see that the men had fallen out on the slope of a hill. Their rifles were piled together in groups of three, and they had begun to eat their breakfast. No sentries had been posted, so they were completely surprised when a group of Germans suddenly appeared and fired at them at short range. Unable to fire back, they retreated in confusion.

Then the Commanding Officer galloped up and ordered Montgomery's battalion to retake the hill. There was no considered plan as to how this should be done, no reconnaissance to determine the strength of the enemy, no covering fire to protect those who were to advance from being mown down.

There were many casualties. The Company Commander was wounded, and, because there were no stretcher bearers to carry him to the dressing station, he was taken prisoner. Montgomery escaped, largely because he tripped and fell over his sword!

The attack failed, and the two companies that had taken part in it returned to their original position and waited for further orders. None arrived. The other companies in their rear had retreated without letting them know. No rations came – Montgomery's sovereigns came in useful here – and the party had to retreat.

For three days they made their way across cornfields, hiding in them by day and moving mainly at night. Their path lay parallel to that of two advancing German lines of troops – and in between them. They were lucky indeed to rejoin their battalion without being killed or captured.

Meanwhile, the Germans had been planning a new sweep along the Belgian coast with the idea of cutting Britain off from the continent of Europe. The British planned to stand firm on a line running south from the Belgian city of Ypres. Montgomery's battalion was ordered to take the village of Meteren.

As the attack began, Montgomery drew his newly sharpened sword and, holding it on high, called on his platoon to follow him. They ran forward towards the village but met with heavy fire. There were many casualties. As they neared the houses, Montgomery was suddenly confronted with a trench full of Germans, one of whom was already aiming at him with his rifle. For a split second Montgomery was at a loss. He had been trained in the use of a bayonet, but no one had explained how one should defend oneself with a sword. Clearly something had to be done – and at once. Montgomery sprang forward towards the German and kicked him as hard as he could in the lower part of the stomach. The German fell to the ground, doubled up with pain, and Montgomery had taken his first prisoner.

But fighting among the houses proved more difficult, and Montgomery was wounded in the chest by a bullet which passed through his right lung. He lay still, hoping that the enemy would suppose him to be dead and not waste any more ammunition on him. But a soldier from his platoon ran to him and began to put a field dressing on his wound. The soldier was shot through the head and fell on top of Montgomery. A German sniper, realising that Montgomery must still be alive, went on firing. A bullet caught him in the knee, giving him a second wound.

Throughout the day no further attempt was made to rescue the two men. But once the village had been taken and darkness fell, the stretcher bearers appeared. Montgomery, though in poor shape, was still breathing and was carried, slung in his greatcoat, for treatment to the Advanced Dressing Station. The doctors did not think he would be likely to survive. In fact they suggested that, as the Dressing Station was due to move on, a grave should be dug for him then and there.

But when the time came to move, Montgomery was still alive. He managed to attract the doctor's attention and was sent back to hospital.

His lung would never be quite the same, and he was out of action for several months, but his tough and wiry constitution allowed him to pull through, and moreover, for himself and his family, there was wonderful news. For he had woken up one morning in hospital to find that for his part in the action at Meteren he had been promoted Captain B. L. Montgomery and had been awarded the Distinguished Service Order medal – a decoration normally limited to those holding the rank of Major or above.

Soon after he left hospital, in January 1915, he was again promoted to be a Staff Officer – a member of the top adminstrative body of the War Office. His task was to help train the citizens' army which was then being formed to support the units of the Regular Army in France and other theatres of war.

Thus, in the short period of six months, an astonishing change had taken place in Montgomery's fortunes. He had faced danger undaunted; he had been dragged back almost from the very jaws of death, and he had his first contacts with civilian recruits of the sort who, a quarter of a century later, would be the muscles and sinews of his never-to-be-forgotten Eighth Army. Above all, he realised that there was a great deal about the art of war that neither he nor the generals leading the British armies had yet learnt.

Left: *A sentry in a trench, 1916.* Right: *A World War I dressing station.* (Imperial War Museum)

After a year, during which the need on the western front for vigorous well-trained officers had become greater than ever before, Montgomery was back in northern France in the area of the River Somme. Further promotion came fast, and by November 1918, when hostilities ended, he was Commanding Officer of 17th Battalion of the Royal Fusiliers. His bravery had been mentioned six times in dispatches.

As soon as the last shot in World War I had been fired, there was a general rush to get back to civilian life. But not all servicemen could be demobilised at once, and Montgomery's task in the days immediately following the Armistice was to keep his men interested in what the Army had still to offer them. He did this by devising training exercises, competitions, discussions and, of course, advice which would help to prepare men for returning to peacetime life at a moment when jobs were becoming harder and harder to find. Once more, he was gaining experience that he would find extremely valuable in the future when dealing with civilians caught up in the war machine.

But even at this time he was something of a rebel.

Montgomery, Commanding 17th Battalion Royal Fusiliers in 1918. On the left is Alan Brooke, also to become a distinguished leader. (Imperial War Museum)

There was so much wrong with the Army. There was, first of all, an enormous gap between the Staff Officers and those in the thick of the fighting. In the field, too, there was a lack of understanding between the men and the generals who commanded them. High-ranking officers seemed to lead an entirely different life from the men they commanded. In his autobiography, Montgomery recalled the story of how Sir Douglas Haig's Chief of Staff, who was about to return to England after some of the heaviest fighting of the War, decided he would like to visit the Passchendaele Ridge over which so much blood had been shed. When he got there and saw the toffee-like mud, flooded trenches and the other terrible handicaps under which the troops had to fight, he could not at first believe it. 'Why wasn't I told?' he asked in horror.

Montgomery's thought was, rather, 'Why hadn't he asked?' or 'Why hadn't he taken the trouble to visit the line earlier?'

What depressed Montgomery at the end of the War was that too many of his contemporaries were all too ready for the Army to revert to the kind of life it had led in peacetime. There was no enthusiasm for reform; no desire to learn the lessons of the War that had just finished – and Montgomery, when he rejoined his regiment again, this time with the modest peacetime rank of a Company Commander, felt that even the senior officers he was likely to meet would be unable to help him in what he hoped would be a serious study of the profession of arms.

But the year before World War I broke out, a man had been posted to Montgomery's battalion who had just finished a two-year course at the Staff College at

Camberley. Captain Lefroy was a bachelor, and was therefore free in the evenings to talk to Montgomery about his favourite subject – how wars should be fought. They used to have long discussions about what was wrong with the Army and how it could be put right, and Lefroy also advised Montgomery on books that were worth reading and on how campaigns should be studied.

It seemed that Camberley was the only place where serious studies of the kind which interested Montgomery were being undertaken. When the College reopened for a shortened course in 1919, Montgomery put his name forward. He was not selected. He applied for the next course. Again his name was passed over.

But he did not give up. Montgomery's regiment was stationed in Cologne, as part of the force which had been ordered to occupy parts of Germany at the end of the War. The Commander-in-Chief at the time was Sir William Robertson. Montgomery had never met him, but he did know that he had begun his career as an ordinary soldier – not as an officer with a commission – and had risen from the ranks by sheer merit. He had had to struggle himself, and Montgomery hoped would be sympathetic to the problems of others. So one afternoon, when he had been invited to play tennis at the Commander-in-Chief's house, Montgomery decided to risk everything and tell the C-in-C of his hopes and how they had been disappointed.

Not long after the tennis party, Montgomery heard that his name had been added to the list, and that he was to report to the Staff College in January 1920. The path to better things was now open.

4

 An Interlude
of Peace

At the Staff College, Montgomery once more was
something of a rebel. As he admitted himself, he was
critical and intolerant, both of his fellow-students
and of the instructors. He believed that the selection
committee had picked the wrong people as students.
And perhaps he was right, for they were supposed to
be the outstanding commanders of the future, yet
very few of them reached top positions in the Army.

One point that mystified Montgomery was that no
one told him whether he had done well or badly
during his year at Camberley: he could not be sure
whether he had made the most of his time among
the exalted.

Meanwhile, although World War I itself was over,
new conflicts had flared up. Southern Ireland, at
that time still a part of the United Kingdom, was
one trouble spot, and the Irish republicans there
were acting much as the IRA do today, organising
hold-ups, raids, ambushes and bank robberies.
Montgomery was posted as Brigade Major to the
17th Infantry Brigade, based on Cork, with instructions to keep order in that area.

Around him, a civil war was raging. The civilian
government was powerless, and the IRA, acting as a
shadow administration, collected whatever revenue
it needed – at gunpoint.

Searching a Post Office waggon, Dublin, 1920. (BBC Hulton)

Police barracks were bombed; magistrates were afraid to hold courts and, in the countryside, the mansions of the English and their sympathisers were burnt to the ground. Montgomery's parents living in Donegal were lucky, as Protestants, to have escaped serious trouble.

When Montgomery arrived, the country was under martial law, but the Army's orders were not to get involved or take sides in the struggle. But if anyone – be he a Republican Army man, a civilian, or even a man wearing police uniform – interfered with an officer or a soldier, he was to be shot at once. How long that policy would have continued to work is uncertain because, by the middle of 1921, the British Government was already seeking to negotiate with the southern Irish to grant them virtual independence. A formal truce was declared between the two sides in July of that year.

In May 1922, Montgomery was posted as Brigade Major to 3rd Division, based on Plymouth, where he was once again concerned with training.

The next year he was posted to the 49th (West Riding) Division in Yorkshire. Up there, he organised his own series of military courses on tactics for junior officers.

His ideas of how wars should be fought had begun to crystallise. Repeatedly, he pointed out that 'steam roller' attacks carried out without an element of surprise could succeed only if the attacking side had many more troops than the defenders. And numbers in themselves need not be the decisive factor. The important thing was to have superiority over the enemy at the point where you intended to strike the decisive blow in a battle.

Apart from this, a commander must explain to the troops he was leading how the battle would be fought. Each unit must know exactly what it was to do, as part of a carefully devised plan in which every risk had been taken into account. All this involved a commander keeping in close contact with the men in his command as well as with its officers. The men should be trained collectively as comrades together in a combined force. Each must realise that his life depends on co-operation with others. It was a lesson that Montgomery himself had learned earlier at some cost, in those early months of the War.

After his spell in Yorkshire, Montgomery was posted back to his regiment, at Shorncliffe Barracks in Kent. Here he found a very different atmosphere. His fellow-officers were interested mainly in horse-riding or similar landed-gentry pastimes. They seemed to have little thought for their work or their profession. Like many people of their day, they believed that the last war was the war to end all wars – and saw no point in preparing for another. To arouse their interest and to add to their knowledge, Montgomery organised a bicycle tour of the battle-fields of northern France. They pedalled all the way.

Possibly Montgomery's enthusiasm got him his next posting – three-year appointment as Instructor at the Staff College at Camberley which he had once found so hard to enter as a pupil. There he con-tinued to air his unpopular belief that set-piece battles in which armies met face to face on a more or less predetermined field of fire were now a thing of the past. What was needed, he kept saying, was mobility, stealth, reconnaissance and deception – and a carefully constructed master plan which would result in a battle being fought in the way you wanted, and not as the enemy would have liked.

*   *   *

In one respect, Montgomery himself was about to perform a 'U-turn'. He had always maintained that, as far as officers were concerned, marriage was not a good thing. 'You must make your choice,' he would insist. 'You can't be both a good soldier and a good husband. It has to be one or the other.'

In the end, he proved himself wrong – though in accordance with a carefully laid master plan.

Up to now, he had shown no interest at all in women. However, it began to be noticed that he was not averse, on the tennis court, to playing in mixed doubles.

In January, 1926, he spent a winter sports holiday

Staff College, Camberley, 1935. (National Army Museum)

in Switzerland and stayed at a hotel in Lenk. He took his skiing seriously and eventually passed the test entitling him to wear the silver 'K' badge of the Kandahar Ski Club. Soon, he was organiser-in-chief of the hotel winter sports. Among the younger skiers that he met and helped at this time were two boys, Richard and John Carver, aged 11 and 12. They were the sons of Mrs Betty Carver, a widow. Her husband had served in the Army and was one of those who lost their lives in World War I.

The following year, Montgomery again went winter sporting at Lenk, and found the Carvers there again. This time, he got to know Betty Carver rather better. Though she had an Army background, she was far from being a typical Army wife. She was not interested in horses, but rather in art, particularly painting and sculpture. She was well-read, and she lived at Chiswick, then the haunt of artists and writers.

None of this daunted Montgomery, for she was

41

also lively and witty. She had great vitality and was extremely popular – and this time Montgomery did not lose touch with her after the holiday was over.

He saw her more and more often when he got back to England, and, for the first and last time in his life, he fell deeply in love. They were married that summer.

Montgomery, of course, left none of the arrangements to the bride, and was even doubtful about whether his father, the Bishop, who was to perform the ceremony, would know what he was about. He also refused to tell the family about any plans for a reception after the wedding. 'The necessary arrangements have been made,' he kept saying.

After the wedding service at Chiswick Parish Church was over and family and friends were standing outside, waiting to be told where to go next, Montgomery and his bride got into their car, waved goodbye, and drove off without more ado on their honeymoon. This was to provide many family jokes.

Montgomery's son David was born the following year, while he was still at Camberley, and most conveniently he had another home posting immediately afterwards – with the job of revising the Army's Infantry Training Manual. For this he was allotted a very pleasant home at Woking. Montgomery naturally insisted on running the house; he ordered the groceries, paid the housekeeping bills, and organised the hospitality.

He did not take his new Army responsibility lightly. He saw it as his job not merely to rewrite the Training Manual but to put into it his views on the role of the infantry and its relationship with the mechanised forces in any future war.

His revisions had, understandably, to be approved by a War Office committee, whose views, as might have been expected, were traditional, and contradictory to his. He, however, refused point blank to accept any alterations by the committee to 'his' book. The final draft, according to Montgomery, contained none of the committee's suggestions. 'The book when published was considered excellent, especially by its author,' he recalled in his *Memoirs*.

*   *   *

After completing 'his' manual, Montgomery was sent as Lieutenant Colonel to command the 1st Battalion of the Royal Warwickshires in Palestine, which Britain at that time ruled under a mandate from the League of Nations, the forerunner of the United Nations. This was a valuable posting, since no officer could expect to rise to the top of his profession without having commanded a battalion of his own regiment.

In January 1931, when Montgomery and Betty arrived in Palestine, the tension was not nearly as great as it became fifteen or so years later. But the Balfour Declaration (Britain's undertaking, given in 1917, that she would look favourably on the establishment in Palestine of a national home for the Jewish people) had already led to fears among the Arabs that they might lose their homeland. In these circumstances, Montgomery's experiences in Ireland proved valuable in dealing both with British officials on the spot and with Arab and Jewish leaders.

Towards the end of the year, however, the battalion was moved to Alexandria, Egypt's main Mediterranean port, not far from the desert in which Montgomery's most famous victory was to be won. Egypt then was of great importance to Britain, since it lay astride the route to India and the Far East, where Britain still ruled Burma, Ceylon (now Sri Lanka) and Malaysia. Italy was at that time in possession of Libya, the territory immediately to the west of Egypt. British troops, when sent to Alexandria, practised manoeuvres in the desert.

It was here that Montgomery put into practice his theory that night attacks need not be limited to small raiding parties. In an army exercise, he carried out a large-scale night attack by the light of flares dropped by aircraft, and won a complete and impressive victory over the 'enemy'.

It might have been a dress rehearsal for the battle he was to fight only ten years later over much the same ground, and his superiors realised that they had in Montgomery an exceptionally talented and enterprising commander in the field.

But, of course, the troops were not out on manoeuvres every week. Their base was the barracks at Alexandria, a city crowded with cafés and bars where soldiers were parted from their money all too easily and with distressing results. Montgomery did his best to provide other interests.

He wrote later, 'I encouraged hobbies of every kind, and one of these was keeping pigeons; this was very popular and we kept some ourselves. One day the quartermaster accused a corporal of having stolen one of his pigeons; the corporal denied the accusation and said the pigeon was his. I had to give judgment. I asked both parties, the quartermaster and the corporal, if a pigeon, when released, would always fly direct to its own loft; they both agreed that this was so. I then ordered the pigeon to be kept for 24 hours in the Battalion Orderly Room. The next day at 10 a.m. I released the pigeon; the whole battalion had heard of the incident and some 800 men watched from vantage points to see what would happen. The pigeon, when released, circled the barracks for a few minutes and then went direct to my own pigeon loft and remained there! This result was accepted by both parties, and the quartermaster withdrew his accusation.'

Early the following year (1934), Montgomery and his battalion were ordered to India where, once again, Montgomery found himself under orders from someone to whom turn-out on parade was more important than efficiency in the field of battle. On one occasion, it is said, orders were given by the Brigade Commander for a ceremonial parade to be held, followed by a march-past in mass formation with the colours trooped and the regimental band playing, to be followed by a general inspection and then a kit inspection in barracks. It was clearly a matter of great importance to the general, and at one point Montgomery himself came under fire.

'Colonel Montgomery,' roared a voice. 'You are not positioned properly in front of your regiment in mass formation. You are six paces too far to your right.'

Montgomery's reaction, according to the legendary story, was immediate. 'Royal Warwickshires,' he cried. 'Six paces right close march.' Thus 700 men moved to the right while Montgomery remained in his original position, which was now correct.

After that spot of bother, the best thing seemed to be to apply for leave, and Montgomery and Betty spent it together in Singapore, Hong Kong, Japan and China. On the way back Montgomery received a telegram from the War Office. It announced that he had been promoted to the rank of full Colonel, and was to become Chief Instructor at the Staff College of the Indian Army at Quetta.

This was a post to which he was very well suited, and he found that being married to Betty was an enormous help. She was popular and unaffectedly friendly towards his colleagues and – still more important in a colonel's wife – she had no favourites. Montgomery entertained a good deal, having come round to the view that, when reporting on an officer, it was useful to know how he behaved off duty as well as how good he was at his work.

Marriage seemed to have mellowed him and outsiders noticed that Betty seemed able to manage him just as she pleased.

This relatively peaceful existence came to an end in May 1935 when a violent earthquake occurred; it lasted barely a minute but affected 3,000 square miles and killed 30,000 people. Betty and David were sent home for a time. But soon after, following his six years abroad, Montgomery was again promoted, to Brigadier, and placed in command of the 9th Infantry Brigade based on Portsmouth.

A large house went with the job – just the right sort of place in which Betty and Monty could unpack their furniture and possessions which they had previously had to leave in storage. There would be room too, for the three boys whenever they were free to come and stay. All seemed set fair.

Top left: *Betty Montgomery, about 1930. All the Field Marshal's personal belongings were destroyed by German bombing in 1941, and this is possibly the only photograph of his wife which survives.* Top right: *Montgomery as Brigade Major, Cork, 1921.* (Col. Brian Montgomery) Centre: *Quetta.* Below: *British troops in Jerusalem, 1929.* (BBC Hulton)

5
 The Shadows
of War

Britain's defences in the mid-1930s, however, were in very poor shape.

The mischief really began in 1919, when the War Cabinet decided, as part of an economy drive, that it would be safe to assume that the British Empire would not be engaged in any major war during the next ten years. By the late 'twenties the shortage of men and equipment had become so serious that on manoeuvres wooden figures were being used to represent officers, and men on horseback were 'tanks'. There was little change up to the end of 1932, at which time efforts were still being made for all-round reduction of expenditure on arms.

In 1933, Ramsay MacDonald, the Prime Minister, proposed that the French should cut their peacetime army from half a million men to 200,000, and that the Germans should be allowed to raise their forces to the same level. That year, the Oxford Union Debating Society passed a resolution to the effect that it would refuse to fight for King and Country. While this was thought to be of little account in Britain, it undoubtedly gave the impression abroad that the British lion no longer had teeth.

The Labour and Liberal parties of the day strengthened this impression by urging all nations to disarm to Germany's level as a prelude to further

Left: *Ramsay MacDonald; his government was largely responsible for Britain's failure to maintain the armed forces between the wars while in Nazi Germany, (right) a compulsory call-up to the army was announced in 1935.* (BBC Hulton)

cuts in arms. But, in 1935, the Germans, in defiance of the Peace Treaty they had signed at the end of the First World War, set up a German air force and decreed a compulsory call-up for the army. This gave the Germans an army of nearly 700,000 troops.

In 1936, Adolf Hitler, the German dictator, felt strong enough to occupy the area bordering the River Rhine and the French frontier, from which German troops had been excluded under the Peace Treaty. Neither Britain nor France took any effective action, a mistake which encouraged Hitler to embark on further military adventures. Thus the chances of war were greatly increased.

Belatedly, Britain had started to build up her own defence forces, but they were pitifully inadequate, and, as late as 1938, the Guards regiments, generally regarded as the elite of the British Army, were drilling with flags to represent machine guns.

This was the situation when Montgomery arrived

home with orders to apply his training methods to his new Brigade. Towards the end of August, he went on manoeuvres on Salisbury Plain, and sent Betty and David to spend the rest of the school holidays at a hotel at Burnham-on-Sea, in Somerset.

And that was where the tragedy occurred. One afternoon on the beach, Betty was stung on the foot by an insect, of what kind no one ever discovered. That evening her leg began to swell and throb; a doctor was called. He sent her to hospital at once, and Montgomery was summoned. But neither the doctor nor the hospital staff could check the spread of the poison.

Blood poisoning set in, and, with misery in his heart, Montgomery could only wait for the end. Betty died in his arms, and was buried at Burnham.

Montgomery was numbed. He had been blissfully happy with Betty, who knew exactly how to treat him.

Now, through a misfortune which could not possibly have been foreseen, he was alone again, his happiness snatched away. 'I seemed to be surrounded by utter darkness,' he afterwards wrote. 'All the spirit was knocked out of me.'

Moreover, he had taken the decision not to worry David by telling him that his mother was ill and in danger of losing her life. He had not wanted him to see her suffer. Now he had to break the news to David that Betty was dead, and to find someone who would look after him both at school and during the holidays. Despite the difference in their ages – Montgomery was 41 years older – the two had to get to know one another better. In time they succeeded, and spent some happy holidays together.

50

Bernard Montgomery and his son, David, 1942. (Col. Brian Montgomery)

After Betty's death, Montgomery took some weeks to recover, but, when he did so, he began to concentrate even more intensely on his military career. There were no longer any distractions; the big house in Portsmouth remained shut up. And the 9th Infantry Brigade soon became known for its alertness and efficiency in the field.

The question of Montgomery's future was settled for him by yet one more promotion. In October 1938, he was raised to the rank of Major-General and given the task of forming a new division out of the units which were then trying to hold down the Arab revolt in Palestine. The situation there was now far more dangerous than at the time of Montgomery's earlier posting. Each year a further quota of Jews had been allowed by the British authorities to enter

Palestine. Wherever possible, they set up communes to which the members, fired with the zeal of pioneers, surrendered all worldly possessions and worked without payment for the common good. Oranges, lemons and grapefruit grown by the *kibbutzim*, as the settlements were called, soon earned a good reputation, and the Promised Land became a land of promise.

Moreover, Hitler's persecution of the Jews in Germany swelled the numbers of those wanting to make a new home in Palestine. There were illegal immigrants as well as legal ones; and some paid vast sums to agents who helped to smuggle them out of Germany, down the Danube, and by sea to the coastline nearest to Jewish communities in Palestine willing to look after them. Most managed to evade the British naval patrols who were trying to stop them.

The Arabs resented the arrival of these well-educated strangers, who spoke a different language, practised a different religion and subscribed to a different culture and outlook on life, particularly with regard to the role of women in society. There were ugly scenes wherever Arabs gathered in the villages and towns. Troops were stoned, windows broken and Jewish shops looted.

Montgomery, however, had arrived just in time to break up the civil war between Jews and Arabs. The army, of course, was hated by both sides for its interference; but firmness paid. A curfew was imposed. Civilian cars moved only when convoyed by the army. Each incident was followed by a reprisal. Villages suspected of aiding terrorists were surrounded without warning, and searched, usually at

Germany stages a military parade in Berlin, 1937, in honour of the Italian leader Mussolini (seen on the dais in a black hat, beside Hitler in a peaked cap). (BBC Hulton)

night. Houses in which arms were found were burnt. Jews and Arabs were treated alike.

The cure began to work and, early in 1939, Montgomery, to his delight, was given a new and more important job.

At a time when the peace of Europe looked even more fragile, he had been selected to command, not a mere Brigade, but the 3rd Division in England, which incidentally contained the 9th Infantry Brigade with which he had been so successful two years earlier at Portsmouth.

But he was very nearly prevented from taking up the post. In May 1939, he fell ill, very suddenly, with a disease that baffled the doctors. He was taken to the Military hospital at Haifa, but there was no improvement in his condition, and friends felt certain that the Army had lost him for good. When he could no longer get out of bed, he was flown to Port Said in the charge of an orderly and two nurses. They were sending him home only because, weak as he was, Montgomery had said again and again that if only he could go home, he would recover.

And, sure enough, once the ship had left port and was ploughing across the open sea, Montgomery began to get better.

When the ship docked at Tilbury he was almost back to normal. Without hanging about, he went for examination by an Army medical board, who pronounced him fit to resume normal duty.

But what was he to do? He could not return to Palestine for, as a casualty, he had already been replaced by a new commander. Yet, with war suddenly so much closer, the War Office considered it would be unwise to disturb the command of the 3rd Division at a time when it might be called on very soon to take part in a general mobilisation. Montgomery was told that he would just have to hang about until a suitable job turned up.

To Montgomery, the War Office decision seemed inexplicable. How could they place on the shelf the man who had written the latest Infantry Training Manual, at the very moment when war was about to break out? And, indeed, the authorities eventually stretched a point and allowed Montgomery to take up command of the 3rd Division – just six days before Hitler's War began.

6

 # The Road to Dunkirk

Montgomery was highly satisfied with his new post, but far from pleased with conditions in the Army. During the 1930s, the same group of ageing generals had clung on to the top positions – playing musical chairs but without taking any of the chairs away, as Montgomery saw it – and the politicians were no better. True, the threat of war had forced them to abandon the belief that no major struggle was to be expected for ten years, and there had been some rearmament. But most of the money was spent on the Navy and Air Force, for the official forecasters clung to the idea that if there were, after all, to be a major war on the Continent, Britain's role would be limited to naval and air support.

Thus when Hitler's War did break out, on September 3rd 1939, and it had become clear that Britain could not afford to stand on the sidelines but would have to support France with a new expeditionary force, the Army was still, as Montgomery put it, perfectly equipped for fighting the war that had broken out in 1914 – a conflict in which men had spent much of their time holding a fixed line of trenches.

Within the War Office, confusion reigned. The three top men – Lord Gort, the Chief of the Imperial General Staff, who was the professional head of the

Army, together with the Director of Military Operations and Intelligence and the Director General of the part-time Territorial Army – were whisked away from their desks and sent overseas, leaving a headless organisation behind them. And Lord Gort, who had been named Commander in Chief of the new British Expeditionary Force, had never before commanded anything larger than an infantry brigade.

The set-up in France was also chaotic. The British contingent, being on French soil, was placed under the command of French generals, and could question the French orders only if they endangered the British Field Force. The British Air Strike Force was not under Gort's command, but he was responsible for maintaining its supplies, through French railways which, like the planes, were outside his control. On top of all this, the French generals disagreed with one another about the right defence tactics.

Meantime Poland had fallen, the western part to the Germans and the eastern part to the Russians, who had also overrun the independent Baltic states of Latvia, Esthonia and Lithuania, and had declared war on Finland. And during the winter months Hitler was planning to seize Norway as well, in order to provide his navy with a new gateway to the Atlantic and to ensure that he could continue to get iron ore supplies from north Sweden without interference from the British Navy. Norway was invaded in April 1940.

Germany had not yet attacked to the west.

Then, on May 10th, German troops poured across the frontiers of Belgium and Holland in what was called a *blitzkrieg*, or lightning war. Taken aback by the speed of the attack, for a few fatal hours the Dutch and Belgians had to face the Germans unaided.

*   *   *

During that first winter of the War, Montgomery, who was in command of the 3rd Division, had been based on Lille, in northern France. He had trained his men hard, concentrating on moving at night.

Once the Germans had invaded Belgium, Montgomery's orders were to advance eastward from Lille into Belgium. His was one of nine divisions on this front.

The real crisis point, it turned out, was not in Belgium at all, but in France, 60 miles south of the British forces, where the German tanks swept through the forests and hills of the Ardennes – rugged and difficult country, which the French had thought to be a natural barrier which no commander would willingly try to cross.

The Germans not only did so, but were soon threatening Paris. Five days after the German attack began, France's Prime Minister, Paul Reynaud, rang to tell Winston Churchill 'We have been defeated'.

That same day, the Netherlands army surrendered.

The British were still holding firm to the north of the line, but now the French armies to the south of it had been slashed to pieces, and there was very little chance of joining up with them again. Another gap appeared between the British and Belgian forces to the left, and Montgomery had to make a night move, side-stepping behind the 5th Division to fill the breach. And at the very time he was moving, the Belgian forces surrendered to the Germans, so by morning there was no one protecting his left flank.

Throughout the crisis, Montgomery's Division had done everything that had been asked of it. But the force would have to be withdrawn to England. The ordeal of Dunkirk had begun.

On May 28th, the 3rd Division moved into a position north of Dunkirk to protect the beaches, from which the troops were being taken off by a fleet of small boats sent across the Channel. Luckily, the weather was calm.

As the size of the force decreased, the senior officers were ordered to appoint substitutes and return home. Montgomery, who had been in charge of a division, was given command of 2nd Corps – a very much larger formation – when General Brooke, its Commander, was recalled. General Alexander was given command of the other remaining Corps, 1st Corps.

On May 30th, Montgomery gave the final orders for withdrawal on to the boats to take place the following night. The bombing had become intense, and some of the hastily built jetties from which men had been embarking had begun to break up. Montgomery and many of his men had to march the six miles to Dunkirk, where the Royal Navy destroyers were still carrying out hazardous rescue work. Montgomery got aboard one at dawn and reached Dover later the same morning.

*   *   *

The evacuation of the British Expeditionary Force from Dunkirk, June 1940: waiting on the beaches to be ferried out by 'small boats' to the Navy ships. (The Times)

The Emperor of India, *a paddle-steamer enlisted by the Navy, brings rescued soldiers safely to Dover.* (Fox Photos)

Though Montgomery had commanded a Corps during the Dunkirk evacuation, he asked to be allowed to return to the 3rd Division ('my 3rd Division', he called it) so that he could re-form and retrain it. By the middle of June he was ready to return to France, where British troops were still fighting. But France surrendered to the Germans on June 17th.

At that time, there were only enough arms and equipment in Britain to fit out one division, and the 3rd Division was chosen as the most deserving.

All kinds of schemes for using it were considered. Its first task was to prepare defences along the south coast of Britain to the west of Brighton. Houses were

Montgomery, as Commander of the South-Eastern Army, inspects a well camouflaged Home Guard. (Fox Photos)

taken over, gardens dug up and machine gun posts set up in them, with barbed wire strung along the sea front.

There were protests from mayors, town councillors and landladies; people were not living in fear of being invaded, and still regarded Dunkirk as an achievement rather than a defeat. Montgomery waved away their objections.

That summer the Prime Minister, Winston Churchill, decided to spend an afternoon with Montgomery's Division. Montgomery was never too pleased at having to spend time with visitors – particularly politicians who, he believed, were at fault for not having equipped the Army properly. But Churchill was different; he at least had warned the country of its peril, though, at the time, few had listened. Churchill was delighted with what he saw.

Less than a month later, Montgomery was promoted again, and placed in command of the 5th Corps, covering Hampshire and Dorset, where his training methods became a model for others to copy. In April of the following year, he was transferred to the even more vital area of Kent, and, in December 1941, was given command of the South-Eastern Army covering Kent, Surrey and Sussex – on the pathway to London. Here, at last, was Montgomery's chance to try out his training methods on the sort of scale that could be decisive in a major war.

7

Wanted: a
General to
win Battles

When he looked around him, Montgomery found
that Britain was suffering, as France had, from
what might be called the Maginot malady – the idea
that you could shelter behind a fixed line of defences
running, in Britain's case, along the coastline.
Others appeared to think that the enemy, once
ashore, could be deterred by a 'scorched earth' policy
– that is, by destroying everything that could be of
value to him. But this made no sense, either, in a
country where distances were so small, and where so
much would have to be destroyed.

Montgomery's approach to the problem was quite
different. In his view, if the Germans succeeded in
setting foot on British soil the plan should be to
attack, not to retreat. His strategy was to man the
coastline itself with light forces, backed by good
radio and telephone communications, so that they
could give headquarters the latest information on
enemy movements and strength. This, in turn,
would allow the main body of troops to direct their
counter-attack to wherever it was most needed. He
reckoned that even light forces on the coast would be
enough to check the enemy attack for a time at least,
and that this would be the moment to attack them –
when they might still be feeling queasy after their
sea crossing.

General Sir Alan Brooke talks to a cross-country runner. (Imperial War Museum)

The set-up would be something like that of a spider's web: no matter where the fly lands, the spider hears of it and rushes to the spot, ready to deal with the intruder.

But this strategy would not succeed unless his troops were fighting fit, and Montgomery saw it as his first task to produce an army that could fight harder and longer than the German invaders. He gave orders that training was to be carried out in all sorts of weather – in rain, snow, over ice and mud, and at any hour of the day or night. The survival of Britain was at stake, and if the Germans could fight well only in fine weather and daylight, and the British could fight under any conditions, then the British were likely to win.

Montgomery had always believed that an army must fight as a single unit and that, from the point of view of fitness, there should be no distinction between those who worked in the administration and those in the front line. Accordingly, he made it a rule that every headquarters in 'his' army, the whole staff under the age of forty, even chaplains and cooks, should turn out once a week and proceed on a seven-mile run. No exceptions were allowed.

He recalled in his *Memoirs* 'the case of a somewhat stout old colonel who went to the doctor and said that if he did the run it would kill him; the doctor brought him to me with a recommendation that he should be excused. I asked him if he truly thought he would die if he did the run; he said yes, and I saw a hopeful gleam in his eye. I then said that if he was thinking of dying it would be better to do it now, as he could be replaced easily and smoothly; it is always a nuisance if officers die when the battle starts and things are inclined to be hectic. He did the run and so far as I know is still alive today'.

In the process of building up his new army, Montgomery concentrated on finding and encouraging the younger officers who showed keenness and an ability to think for themselves. Older officers who had been called up after semi-retirement, some of whom had never seen any fighting and were not sure whether they could rise to the occasion, were got rid of. When Montgomery carried out an inspection, his custom was to make the men take off their steel helmets; this was not, as some people might have thought, to see if their hair had been properly cut, but to see if they had the light of battle in their eyes.

This policy of weeding out the inefficient and lazy made him many enemies.

Even more controversial was his decision to banish wives and families of officers who had come to live near their husbands in the critical invasion area. His argument was that, if an officer's family were with him or near him at the time an invasion took place, he would be tempted to see to their safety before turning his attention to the enemy.

*   *   *

Throughout this critical time, Montgomery never lost a chance to explain what he was trying to do. He talked to senior officers and junior officers, both singly and in groups. He was one of the few leaders who had something new to say.

Having worked as an instructor both at Camberley and Quetta Staff Colleges, he found no difficulty in explaining his views simply and clearly. He always spoke quietly and seldom raised his voice. Smoking and coughing were frowned on, because they interfered with the concentration of his audience. And those who were late, even by a minute, were often made to wait outside until Montgomery had finished the first half of his lecture.

All this did not add to Montgomery's popularity within the army, but it did add considerably to the confidence of those whom he was protecting. They came to realise that even if his South-Eastern Army was not stretched along the coastline and might have to lose some towns and villages at the start of an invasion, this was because it was more important to smash the German army than it was to retain every inch of territory.

Meanwhile, the chances of an invasion taking

place had gradually decreased. The Battle of Britain, fought in the air over the English Channel and the southern counties, had proved that the German air force did not have the superiority needed to guarantee that their forces could approach the English coast without crippling losses on the way; and those that did succeed in landing could not be guaranteed air cover.

Other theatres of war began to receive more attention – particularly the Middle East which, then as now, provided much of the Army's oil and petrol.

*   *   *

Libya, including the area eastwards to the Egyptian border, was still ruled by Benito Mussolini, the Italian dictator, and there was a real danger that German and Italian forces would press on eastwards from Libya into Egypt, and thence onwards to the Middle East oilfields in Iran, Iraq and elsewhere. The British, Australian, New Zealand and Indian troops had already made three attempts at clearing the enemy out of North Africa. Each had failed.

In February 1941, the Italians had been driven out of Egypt across 750 miles (1200 kms) of desert to the west. Perhaps they might have been content to stay there if a German general (later a Field Marshal) of great daring and ability had not come on the scene. He was Erwin Rommel.

Now Rommel was putting new courage into the Italians, and in April 1941, using a certain amount of bluff and a great deal of energy, he succeeded in regaining almost all the ground that had been lost earlier in the year.

66

Commanders-in-Chief, Middle East. Top left: *Auchinleck,* (top right) *Alex-ander,* (below left) *Wavell.* Below right: *Their chief adversary; the German general, Erwin Rommel.* (Imperial War Museum)

At this point, General Wavell, Commander in Chief in the Middle East, was removed and replaced by General Auchinleck. He in turn made a new attack on Rommel in November 1941. But this action, too, was only partially successful. Auchinleck planned to make an attack in June, but, unfortunately, Rommel beat him to the punch. He attacked in May, and inflicted another severe defeat on the Eighth Army. Cairo was within range of fighter aircraft. The Royal Navy's larger warships were hastily moved from the Mediterranean to the safety of the Red Sea, and Mussolini prepared to enter the Egyptian capital in triumph.

In the meantime, British forces had been defeated by the Germans in both Greece and Crete and, in the Far East, a Commonwealth force of orginally more than 70,000 men had surrendered in Singapore to the Japanese.

In the House of Commons, Winston Churchill had to face a vote of censure on the central direction of the War. MPs supported him by a vote of 475 to 25; but it was clear that the time had come for another change of command in the Middle East.

Up to that time Auchinleck, like Wavell, had been in command of an area stretching from Egypt to the borders of India. Churchill's solution was to split the area into two, giving Auchinleck the eastern part. For the western part, that is mainly Egypt and Libya, he chose General Alexander. Under him, in charge of the Eighth Army, would be Lieutenant General Gott.

At that time, Alexander was otherwise engaged. The United States had now joined in the war, following the Japanese attack on Pearl Harbor and joint Anglo-American landings code-named 'Torch' were being planned in Algeria and Morocco. These would meet in part the Russian call for a Second Front against the Germans and as well as helping the British in North Africa. Alexander had already been chosen as Commander of the 'Torch' Task Force which was due to land in November 1942 – only three months away. Now that Alexander was no longer available for 'Torch', Churchill looked round for a substitute, and chose Montgomery.

Montgomery was watching a large-scale exercise in Scotland when he was recalled to London by the War Office and told that he would now be replacing Alexander, working under General Eisenhower on 'Torch'. At 7 o'clock the following morning, while he was shaving, the War Office telephoned again. The plans had been changed overnight.

General Gott had died in a 'plane crash, and Montgomery was now to forget 'Torch' and to take over the Eighth Army. He was to fight Rommel, who had defeated so many British commanders before. In the few hours left to him, he arranged for his son David to be looked after by friends. Then he flew off with a light heart. He would be serving under Alexander, whom he had known and admired since they commanded twin Corps together on the beaches of Dunkirk.

Together, he felt sure they would drive out the Germans. In Montgomery's words, 'Rommel would be headed off, then seen off, then written off'.

8

 Desert
Victory

Montgomery arrived in Cairo on August 12th, 1942, a sweltering day, still wearing his thick serge UK Service uniform. His first appointment (after taking a bath) was with the outgoing commander, General Auchinleck. The two had met in the past without seeing eye to eye. Their feelings that day in Cairo were no more friendly than before.

By this time, the British front had been established along a line running from the sea southwards for about 45 miles (say 70 kms) to a part of the desert known as the Quattara Depression, a vast salt marsh impassable except, in a few places, by camels. The Germans had been held back on this line, but only just, and, although Auchinleck was planning a counter-attack, he was prepared to withdraw all his troops out of Egypt altogether rather than see the Eighth Army destroyed as a fighting force.

This was not the way to beat Rommel, Montgomery felt. That very afternoon, Montgomery began making plans to assemble a secret armoured mobile striking force like the Panzer Division that Rommel had used with such success.

Next morning at 5 o'clock he set out for the desert to see conditions for himself. He had asked Freddie de Guingand, then Brigadier, General Staff of the Eighth Army, to show him the way to headquarters.

Left: *A section of British barbed wire defences in the desert.* Right: *'Freddie' de Guingand, Montgomery's Chief of Staff from 1942 till the end of the War. Montgomery left all detailed planning to him.* (Imperial War Museum)

They were old friends, and Montgomery knew he could rely on him for an accurate account of how things were going.

As was to be expected after two defeats and as many changes of command, morale in the Eighth Army was poor. Obviously a shake-up from top to bottom was needed, and Montgomery thought that it was now or never. He decided not to wait for the formal hand-over ceremonies due in two days' time but to take over command at once. After lunch, he coolly informed GHQ in Cairo that he had assumed command of the Eighth Army from 2 p.m. All previous orders based on the assumption of a withdrawal from the desert were cancelled.

During the afternoon, Montgomery saw both the Australian and New Zealand Corps Commanders, to make the new system work.

That evening, he met his headquarters staff. He appeared before them in desert uniform with shorts,

71

which his aide had managed to get for him that day in Cairo; but his white knees proclaimed him as a newcomer to the desert sun.

Montgomery's speech to the officers at head-quarters was short and to the point. 'I want first of all to introduce myself to you,' he said. 'You do not know me. I do not know you. But we have got to work together; therefore we must understand each other, and we must have confidence in each other . . .

'Now let me tell you the general lines on which we will work. I believe that one of the first duties of a commander is to create what I call "atmosphere". I do not like the general atmosphere I find here. It is an atmosphere of doubt, of looking back to select the next place to which to withdraw, of loss of confidence in our ability to defeat Rommel, of desperate defence measures by reserves in preparing new positions in the Cairo area and the Delta [of the Nile]. All that must cease. Let us have a new atmosphere. The defence of Egypt lies here at Alamein . . . What is the use of digging trenches in the Delta? It is quite use-less. If we lose this position we lose Egypt.' Mont-gomery then declared that all the fighting troops now in the Delta would have to come out to the desert at once. There would be no further with-drawal.

At the same time, plans would be made for a great offensive. 'It will be the beginning of a campaign which will hit Rommel and his army for six right out of Africa. I have no intention of launching our great attack until we are completely ready; there will be pressure from many quarters to attack soon; *I will not attack until we are ready*, and you can be assured on that point.'

Montgomery added that it was essential that the new atmosphere in which the army would work and fight should permeate right down to the most junior private soldier. All the soldiers must know what was wanted. When they saw it coming to pass there would be a surge of confidence throughout the Army.

Montgomery's system of control was also new to them. He at once appointed de Guingand as his Chief of Staff, and explained that in future de Guingand would issue the orders which were to be treated as if they had come from Montgomery himself. And there was to be no 'belly-aching'.

Montgomery's reason for de Guingand's appointment was that he needed time to think out not only the next battle but the one after next. Then he could tell de Guingand what he had decided and leave him to carry out the details of the plan. All communications were to pass through de Guingand.

To keep in touch throughout the day, Montgomery appointed a number of young liaison officers to keep him up-to-date with developments in all critical sectors on the battlefield and to see that his orders were being carried out.

*   *   *

Montgomery was astonished when he first arrived in the desert and was shown Auchinleck's headquarters. It was a structure of tubular pipes covered with mosquito netting. 'What's this? A meat-safe?' he asked. 'Surely you don't expect me to live in a meat-safe, do you? Take it down and let out the poor flies.' It appeared that Auchinleck, in his desire to see that officers in the desert were no more comfortable than the men, had installed misery for all. Auchinleck himself had slept on the ground outside his caravan; there were no tents. Officers ate in the open in the sun. The mosquito netting, which provided no shade, was the only concession to very senior officers. The only trouble was that the headquarters was so primitive that it couldn't keep in permanent touch with Cairo or anywhere else.

Moreover, it was many miles away from the Air Force headquarters, which had been set up on the shores of the Mediterranean. It was as if the two commanders had been fighting different wars.

Montgomery's solution was to move his main headquarters up to the coast, where it could keep in close touch with the Royal Air Force. He allowed tents, to be set up. There was swimming for those who wanted. 'Let us all be as comfortable as we reasonably can,' Montgomery urged.

He himself kept clear of main headquarters, with its stream of visitors and other distractions, and set up a small mobile Tactical HQ, with a small staff of signals, cipher clerks, liaison officers, defence troops and an operations staff.

And as an aid to defeating the enemy, he kept a photograph of Rommel pinned above his desk in his caravan. He studied the face, and tried to think into his enemy's mind. Equally unconventionally, he kept a canary to entertain him.

As far as possible, Montgomery kept to a set daily routine. He was awake at 6 a.m. for a cup of tea and spent the next half hour or so on considering the best tactics for overcoming the enemy, deciding what was possible, planning the instructions he intended to give and visits he meant to pay during the day. By

8.30, he had had breakfast and had set out in his car to visit Corps headquarters, and was usually back at his own headquarters for tea. Between then and dinner, he would be in touch with both de Guingand at Main Headquarters and the Corps Commanders, setting out plans for the next day. De Guingand would then hold his own group conference for the arrangements for carrying out Montgomery's orders. After dinner, Montgomery would listen to the reports of his liaison officers. Soon afterwards he would write his diary, go to bed with a novel, and sleep soundly.

For years, he had followed much the same time-table. He made it a rule that he was not to be woken up at night except in the direst emergency.

Montgomery, photographed in 1946, in one of his caravans, with pictures of three of his famous enemies: Rommel, Himmler and Doenitz. (Fox Photos)

Montgomery had always believed that the most important factor in a battle is the morale of the individual soldiers fighting it. Victories, he used to say, are won in the hearts of men, before the first shot is fired. But the soldier's morale, that confidence he has in himself and his weapons, depends largely on his commander. It is for the commander to win that confidence, and the first step towards doing so is to make himself known to his troops.

Montgomery had his own methods of doing so. In the blackout of France, his car had been fitted with a distinctive coloured light. In the desert, he first borrowed a broad-brimmed hat from an Australian unit so that he could be distinguished more easily. Later, however, while watching a battle action from a tank, he was offered a beret as being more practical. He accepted it and added his own General's badge to that of the Royal Tank Corps. He was recognised – the tank general without the tank – wherever he showed himself.

He realised from the start that he was dealing with civilians in uniform who had never planned to join the Army, Navy or Air Force, and who were not used to military ways. They could be inquisitive and critical. They liked to know not only the aims of the campaign but what part they were playing in it and how they were contributing to its success. They liked to see their commanding officer, and be taken notice of by him, and Montgomery, wherever possible, met their wishes.

The men felt that they were important to him and that he studied their interests. Thus when Churchill asked him what he could do to reward the magnificent men of the Eighth Army, he was ready at once with the right answer: improve the mail services so that the troops could get the latest news from home and keep in touch with their families.

But he was quick to see that only victories in the field of battle could build up lasting confidence between the troops and their commander. His chance came when Rommel attacked a mere fortnight after Montgomery had taken over command. The attack had been expected, and Montgomery had spent much time in reasoning out what form it would take.

*   *   *

The southern end of the British line rested, it will be remembered, on the edge of a vast and impassable salt marsh, the Quattara Depression, and it seemed likely, as this was the less strongly held part of the line, that Rommel would attack there.

This being so, Montgomery decided that the best way to defeat Rommel was to allow him to advance along the edge of the marsh, past the southern end of the British line, and then attack his flank. The British attack would be made at the point where Rommel had to pass between the marsh and a piece of rising ground known as Alam el Halfa. But this would not be one of those swirling, fast-moving engagements of the kind which Rommel loved to fight – with tanks of each side racing round each other for the best position. On the contrary, most of the Eighth Army tanks were ordered to dig themselves into concealed positions and stay there. Montgomery concealed a sizeable number of them behind the brow of Alam el Halfa. They were to be used as

77

artillery to smash Rommel's forces as soon as the enemy came within range. His advance along the side of depression would, of course, be hindered by minefields and soon he would meet with the tanks of the 7th Armoured Division, the famous 'Desert Rats'. But their orders were to retire before him, doing as much damage as possible. They were not to engage in a tank battle; their job was to lure him onwards towards Alam el Halfa. Landmines, signals, tank workshops, hospitals, ammunition supplies and water – all had to be transferred to new positions to suit the new plan.

To Montgomery's great satisfaction, the battle proceeded exactly as he had foreseen. The Eighth Army stood firm; Rommel was forced to fight a set-piece encounter in which his forces were constricted by the natural obstacles of the marsh, and the hill, and of course the 'Desert Rats'. He tried to storm the hill but was repulsed. After the battle of Alam el Halfa had raged for six days he was compelled to withdraw with heavy losses.

The effect on the Eighth Army can well be imagined. Here was a general who had told them there would be no withdrawal and there *was* no withdrawal – except by Rommel. Things were looking up at last. Admittedly, there was no attempt to pursue Rommel's army. But there were good reasons for this. Montgomery was determined to save his armour for the major battle that would soon have to be fought. He wanted to keep the Germans and Italian divisions in their present position – far from base at the end of a long supply line, and therefore shorter than ever of petrol.

But just how should the great battle be fought?

What was the master plan to be? As that summer of 1942 drew to a close, the two armies faced one another in more or less parallel lines. In the desert, with no real cover, it was difficult to hide the fact that an attack was being got ready. The best that Montgomery could do was to conceal as far as possible the timing of the attack and where he intended to strike the main blow. He decided to go north of the centre of the enemy line – so that, once he had pierced it, he would be free to turn either further north or south, according to the circumstances at the time. He was also determined that the battle should be fought towards the end of October, when the full moon would allow the infantry to clear a path more easily through the enemy minefields.

Montgomery's headquarters were set up near El Alamein, a railway station at a point where the line runs close to the sea. But he intended the enemy to think that the main thrust would come at the opposite end of the line – in the south. He constructed a dummy fuel pipeline and one for water leading to the southern sector of the front. He stepped up the number of radio messages sent and received there. Also the dummy lines were constructed at a rate which allowed the Germans to suppose that they would be completed by mid-November – two or three weeks later than he intended to attack.

The deception was so successful that Rommel thought it safe to leave the front and fly to Austria for treatment for his internal catarrh, and, a few hours before the battle commenced, Rommel's deputy reported that the day had been a normal one. Montgomery had arranged for his attack to begin on the night of October 23rd. He reasoned that, if he attacked at night, the enemy would be forced to make their counter-attack by day – with less chance of springing a surprise on the Allied troops.

*   *   *

Montgomery's forecast of how things would go seems, with hindsight, to have been uncannily accurate. This is what he said on the day before:

'My forecast of this battle is that there will be three definite stages: the break-in to the enemy's positions, the dog-fight, the break-out. We will do the break-in on the night of 23rd October. The dog-fight battle will then begin and will involve hard and continuous fighting . . . I believe that the dog-fight battle will become a hard killing match and will last for ten to twelve days . . . It will be absolutely vital during this period to retain the initiative and to force Rommel to dance to our tune *all the time*; we must all keep going however tired we may be. . . .

'After the dog-fight has gone on for about ten to twelve days, the enemy will crack. Then will come the break-out, and that will lead to the end of Rommel in Africa . . .'

Montgomery's Order of the Day to his troops read, 'When I assumed command of the Eighth Army I said that the mandate was to destroy Rommel and that it would be done as soon as we were ready.

'We are ready *now*. The battle that is about to begin will be one of the decisive battles of history. It will be the turning point of the war. The eyes of the world will be on us, watching anxiously which way

Camouflage in the desert: a dug-out, a cookhouse, heavy guns. (Imperial War Museum)

the battle will swing. We can give them our answer at once: it will swing our way.

'We have first class equipment; good tanks; good anti-tank guns; plenty of artillery and plenty of ammunition; and we are backed by the finest air striking force in the world. All that is necessary is that each one of us, every officer and man, should enter into the mighty battle with the determination to see it through – to fight and to kill – and finally, to win. If we do this, there can only be one result – together we will hit the enemy for "six" right out of North Africa.'

That evening at 9.40, the barrage of a thousand guns began. Within a short while, the main communications system of the main German headquarters had been knocked out. They had no idea where to meet the attack.

Montgomery, as usual, had gone to bed by this time and was sleeping well. But the next morning, things did not look nearly as good. In general, the master plan was for the infantry to clear a path through the enemy minefields, through which the tanks would then pass. But the minefields proved to be deeper and more complex than was expected. The infantry fell behindhand with their work and got in the way of the armoured columns that were following. Dawn broke before the tanks could get clear. Some tank commanders thought of withdrawing until darkness fell again, but Montgomery insisted that the tanks should give the enemy no respite; they must fight their way out without further help from the infantrymen. This proved difficult and the British armoured divisions had still not broken clear by nightfall on October 24th.

On October 25th, Montgomery recognised that, for the moment, it was impossible for two of his armoured divisions to advance any further. Little progress was made that day or the next, and Montgomery had to rethink his next move.

*   *   *

He was in an awkward position. He had no reserves of infantry, and he had already lost as many tanks in the battle as the enemy had possessed at the start. It would take time to recover those that had been temporarily disabled. His forces would have to be regrouped if they were to strike the final blow, and after such heavy fighting a rest-pause might be valuable.

Between October 26th and 28th, Montgomery pulled both the New Zealand 2nd Division and the 1st Armoured Division from their place in the front line, replacing them by defensive troops. When London got the news of this, there was consternation. Churchill complained that Montgomery was 'dragging his feet'. On October 29th, Alexander, the Commander in Chief, hurried down from Cairo to see what was wrong. With him came Robert Casey, the Australian politican who had been appointed Minister of State in the Middle East.

But Montgomery succeeded in reassuring both his visitors. He would soon be ready to make the final assault which would send Rommel reeling back.

He had originally intended to concentrate his new attack in the north of the front near the coast, where road and rail communications were good. But he learnt from his Intelligence staff that the Germans

Montgomery watches his men pursue the fleeing Afrika Korps. (Imperial War Museum)

had just transferred some of their best troops to that sector. So he decided, instead, to attack at the weakest point in the line, the part where the Italian and German forces shared the front.

The final attack, code-named 'Supercharge', began at 01.05 in the morning of November 1st and lasted for three more days. Once more, the losses were heavy at the start, and the 9th Armoured Brigade alone lost 87 tanks. But in the end, numbers told. A furious curtain of shells helped to clear a corridor through the enemy minefields.

And, this time, there was no need for the mine clearing squads to stake out the channels they had cleared with tape and lights. A continuous line of tracer ammunition on each side of the channel showed the way forward. And then, at last, through the swirling dust came the rumble of tanks. By the afternoon of November 4th, they had burst through the enemy lines and were ranging across the desert. That afternoon Rommel, who had flown back from Austria in the hope of stemming the tide, gave the order to retreat. He had then fewer than 60 tanks against more than ten times that number. After thirteen days, hardly a day longer than Montgomery had predicted, the battle of El Alamein was over.

Thirty thousand men, nearly a third of the original enemy force, had been taken prisoner, and possibly another 20,000 killed or wounded. Rommel had to leave behind 1,000 guns and 450 tanks. Others fell by the wayside during his withdrawal. The Italians alone had to abandon 75 of their tanks when they ran out of petrol.

Critics might say that the victory was neither absolute nor complete, as Montgomery claimed, since Rommel lived to fight another day, and that Montgomery was exaggerating in order to build up his own importance. Nevertheless, if he convinced the Eighth Army that they were indomitable, he was doing what good generals should do and had previously failed to do: raise morale at home and in the desert.

The victory was in any case perfectly timed. It more or less coincided with the successful Anglo–American landings on the coast of Morocco and Algeria – and allowed the Navy to take supplies once more to the beleaguered island of Malta.

As soon as Churchill heard the news, he gave orders for the church bells of Britain to be rung. For three years they had been held in reserve, silenced – for use only as an alarm if the enemy had landed. Now they could sound again, for in a single battle Montgomery and his Eighth Army had shown both President Roosevelt in Washington and Generalissimo Stalin in Moscow that Britain was now a reliable and even a powerful military ally.

9

 # The
Path to Rome

In just a few days, Montgomery had become world-famous. Here was the general that everybody had been waiting for, all through the defeats of the previous three years – a general who could not only promise victory but achieve it; a commander who cared enough for the troops to come round and see them; a leader who trained them in a hard school because that was the way to save lives – their lives. The Eighth Army had made a name for itself and for all who served with it. His troops were never to lose a major battle from the time Montgomery arrived in Egypt, in August 1942, till he accepted the surrender of the opposing German forces, in May 1945.

Yet the twelve months between November 1942 and December 1943, the period immediately following El Alamein, were among the least rewarding of his career. He had first of all to drive Rommel back across a thousand miles of desert, in order to capture the vital port of Tripoli. Then, he had to battle his way across the frontier into Tunisia and past barriers which the French had been fortifying for years as a safeguard against invasion.

In the struggle to capture Tunis, he had to cooperate with the American commanders, who, he felt, 'did not know my ways'. True, they had landed successfully on the North African coast, but

Montgomery had his doubts about whether they could fight. Their troops were not yet accustomed to do without peacetime comforts and had never been hardened in battle.

It was hoped that the American forces would attack and capture the city of Tunis from the west, across flat and open country. But unfortunately the attack was mounted on too broad a front ('a partridge drive' was how Montgomery described it) and was beaten off with heavy loss.

Montgomery had to send two divisions and one of his own generals, to arrange for a new, concentrated attack. It was a success, and Montgomery's 7th Armoured Division led the way into Tunis with the American troops following. Some humorist even rigged up a sign at the entrance to the city reading 'Eighth Army welcomes First Army to Tunis'. The men of the American First Army did not see the joke, but at least, now that the British and American forces had joined one another, the war in Africa was over and it was time to plan for the invasion of the island of Sicily, lying off the toe of Italy. The liberation of Europe would then have begun.

*   *   *

Once again, however, there were differences between Montgomery and the American commanders.

Despite rough weather and the fact that some of the British forces and their equipment had to be brought from ports as far away as Haifa (Palestine) and Alexandria, the landings, the first of which took place on July 10th, were successful. From then on the going became difficult. Within three days, Hitler decided to send two more divisions into Sicily. The countryside, though picturesque enough with its vineyards and orange groves, was 'close' – that is, good ambush country. There were numerous bridges, which the Germans took care to blow up. So Montgomery's progress up the east coast of the island was rather slow – too slow for the Americans.

He had never thought that Sicily would be an easy conquest. General George Patton, Commander of the US 7th Army, had declared that the task would be a simple one. And, from his point of view, it was.

Patton was a great believer in high-speed advance, even though it could mean running ahead of the supplies he needed. And on this occasion he was proved right, to the extent that he was able to enter the city of Messina, the nearest port to Italy, some hours before Montgomery got there. And this was after he had already captured Sicily's largest city, Palermo, at the other end of the island.

Montgomery was far from pleased at this turn of events. His view was that it was a mistake for Patton to have wasted time in capturing Palermo. He should have concentrated instead on preventing the Germans getting out of Sicily and over to Italy.

But friction between the British and Americans was not confined to the field of battle. Earlier in the year, in Tunisia, there had been the incident of the Flying Fortress.

Montgomery's story was that General Eisenhower's Chief of Staff, General Bedell Smith, had been discussing how soon the British and American forces could join up. Montgomery said he could reach Sfax, the proposed meeting place, by April 15th. Bedell Smith's reply was that if Monty could do that,

Left: *General George S. Patton, Commander of the US 7th Army, later Commander of the 3rd Army in Normandy, who never got on with Montgomery.* Right: *Montgomery and Eisenhower (Commander-in-Chief, Allied Forces in North Africa).* (Imperial War Museum)

General Eisenhower would give him anything he liked to ask for. Montgomery said 'That's a deal', adding that he would like an American airplane for his own use.

When British troops entered Sfax, five days early on April 10th, Monty sent a message: 'Entered Sfax 08.30 this morning. Please send Fortress'. (The Flying Fortress was then the jumbo of the US bomber fleet.)

Bedell Smith had thought that Montgomery was leg-pulling when they made the deal, and had not let Eisenhower in on the joke. Eisenhower responded nobly, but he was not amused.

*   *   *

With his own troops, Montgomery's popularity remained undimmed. A group of soldiers battling to repair a bridge would see a staff car, and in it the unmistakable figure of Montgomery. The car would

89

stop and 'Monty' would spring out. At a gesture from him the men would cluster round.

'What unit is this?' he would ask, and on being told would comment, as like as not, 'Ah yes, one of the finest. We shall need this bridge of yours to send the Germans reeling backwards. This is our first away match on the continent of Europe and we must win it. We're going to hit the Germans for six; *and* the Italians. See them both off. Make them score an own goal. But mustn't forget. Plenty of lemons here, but no half-time interval. Have to go on till we finish. By the way, do any of you smoke? You do? Well, some cigarettes will be handed out.' Then back to the staff car and away.

Montgomery's prediction that the enemy would soon be scoring own goals might mean nothing to a general, but to the average soldier it meant everything.

Montgomery's critics in the Army were largely to be found among the officer class. There were several reasons for this. One was that Montgomery regarded most, indeed all, officers with a critical eye. His own view was that there were no bad regiments, only bad officers. And he was quite ruthless with those who did not come up to his standards. 'I am afraid you are quite useless as far as I am concerned. Totally useless,' he would declare to anyone he proposed to transfer to another theatre of war. It did not win him friends among the junior and middle-ranking officers.

Nor was he popular among senior officers. They saw Montgomery's action in seizing command of the Eighth Army from Auchinleck two days in advance of the official handover as a slight to the outgoing commander.

He was not over-popular with the Royal Navy who, in his view, had been sluggish in getting supplies through the ports that had been captured from the enemy. His remark: 'We need people who can open harbours – not bottles,' soon got back to naval wardrooms and was not forgotten.

The Army and Air Force differed both on strategy – what the master plan should be – and on tactics – how the plan should be carried out. In general, the Air Force commanders wanted a plan that would give them the maximum number of airfields in the shortest possible time. For Montgomery, on the other hand, the most important job was to manoeuvre so as to destroy the enemy's armour and infantry with as few casualties as possible. If he succeeded in that, the airfields would fall as well.

Success in wartime made Montgomery more enemies than he had ever had in the days of peace. 'Quick as a ferret and about as lovable,' his critics said.

His system of showing himself as often as possible to as many as possible – which he considered a vital factor in building up morale – was thought by his critics to be a piece of self-advertisement. He was told he was not entitled to wear a Tank Corps beret, and was ordered to cease doing so. He rejected the order, and said that the beret was worth two extra divisions.

*   *   *

He really needed them when the time came for the Eighth Army to leave Sicily for Italy. For once again there were differences between the British and the

Americans, not only at Montgomery's level but higher up.

Churchill and his advisers saw the Italian campaign as a way of attacking the 'soft under-belly' of the enemy from the security of the foothold the Allies already had in Sicily. The Americans, on the other hand, considered the invasion of Italy as useful but not decisive. The real liberation of Europe would not take place, they felt, until the Germans had been driven out of France, Belgium, the Netherlands and other western democracies. They preferred to treat Italy as a holding operation that would keep German troops tied down while they prepared the much more important landings to be mounted from Britain across the Channel, and in the south of France.

Perhaps they were right, for both British and American forces found Italy a tough proposition. Each mountain – and there were hundreds of them – seemed to have a stream running down from it, over which there was a bridge, which the Germans had succeeded in blowing up before the Allied forces could get across.

As it was, the autumn drew on, and sunny Italy, the land of chickens, melons and wine, turned into a general's nightmare, with heavy rainstorms and piercing cold winds, and mud which slowed and sometimes stopped the tanks.

At the beginning of November, a final attempt

Opposite: Top; *Generals Leese, Montgomery and Simonds (of the Canadian Army), hold a conference in Sicily.* (Imperial War Museum)
Centre: *Good ambush country around Taormina, Sicily.* (Imperial War Museum)
Below: *The Eighth Army is welcomed in Catania, Sicily.* (Imperial War Museum)

was made to break the German winter line behind the Sangro River and open up the highway from Pescara to Rome.

Pescara was still 16 miles away as Christmas drew near. In a few days there would be snow, and there would be no more campaigning till the spring – and no chance of taking Rome or breaking through to the plains of Lombardy. Montgomery's run of successes seemed to have petered out.

But his luck held; early on the morning of December 24th, he was woken and given a signal from the War Office. It ordered him to return to England to take charge of the 21 Army Group, the cluster of armies that were to land on the beaches of Normandy and free the rest of Europe from German occupation. So instead of stagnation, there was promotion.

*   *   *

It had been touch and go whether he was given the job. True, 'Monty', as he was now almost universally called, was highly popular with the average citizen. His beret was known far and wide, and, when he went to the theatre, he stopped the show.

His success began to worry the politicians. Would Montgomery turn into another Cromwell, or perhaps a military dictator, they asked themselves. In the clubs, it was said that Churchill had described him as 'in defeat unthinkable; in victory insufferable' . . . that Montgomery's staff were forced to attend prayers twice a day and dared not cough while Montgomery read the lessons . . . that someone who asked how the battle was going was told:

'According to plan: it began at 6 a.m., and Monty sacked the Corps Commander at ten.' Military men recalled that Montgomery had once said in the mess, 'You have to be a bit of a cad to get on in the Army, and I am a bit of a cad,' and had sounded rather proud of the fact.

The Americans did not want to serve under him, and the Cabinet urged Churchill to appoint Alexander, who was a born diplomat as well as a fine general, to the post. Montgomery was particularly unpopular with the Canadians, whose Commander-in-Chief, General McNaughton had journeyed all the way from Malta to see the Canadian troops fighting in Sicily and had been forbidden to do so by Montgomery until the fighting was over. But, in the end, the decision was that the landings on the Continent would be such an unusual operation, involving many risks that could not be foreseen, that the commander chosen must be not only a supreme organiser, and a man of ingenuity and enterprise, but someone capable of raising the morale of the troops to the point where they could face the unknown with confidence – Montgomery.

On his way home he called on Churchill, then in Morocco, and the great man wrote in his autograph book: 'The immortal march of the Eighth Army from the gates of Cairo along the African shore through Tunisia, through Sicily, has now carried its ever-victorious soldiers and their world-renowned commander far into Italy towards the gates of Rome. The scene changes and vastly expands. A great task accomplished gives place to a greater in which the same unfailing spirit will win for all true men a full and glorious reward. Winston S. Churchill.'

10

 The Battle
for Normandy

Here was real power. Montgomery was now in command, not merely of a single army, but of a group of armies, including the US 1st Army under General Omar Bradley. Within eight weeks of landing, he would have under his command more than 900,000 Americans, 800,000 British, a budding Canadian army and 365,000 vehicles – one to every five men. And for all this he would be responsible to only one man – General Eisenhower. The plan, appropriately was given the code-name 'Overlord'.

There had already been a good deal of discussion on where the landings should take place. They would have to be made near enough to airfields in Britain to allow the Air Force to give the troops fighter cover. Also, the beaches where the troops landed would have to be flat. So the area chosen was the large bay in Normandy sheltered from the worst of the Atlantic weather by the Cotentin Peninsula, a jagged tree-stump of land pointing northward from the French coast in the direction of Bournemouth.

The choice of Normandy was a good one, but, having agreed to this, Montgomery at once began to ask 'What's the plan?' How was the landing, if successful, to be exploited? Where would the main blows be struck, and with what object?

As usual, he stripped the problem down till only

the essentials remained. His master plan was to draw the bulk of the Germans into a hard-fought battle on one side of the Peninsula, the east side round the city of Caen, leaving the Americans free to capture the port of Cherbourg in the north and to break out of the Peninsula along the west side.

Once the general strategy had been agreed, Montgomery left it to his staff (based in St Paul's, his old school) to work out the details, while he himself concentrated on raising the morale and self-confidence of the troops.

In the weeks that followed, he talked to more than a million soldiers – Norwegians, Canadians, Poles, Belgians and the Free French who would be with him in the battle, as well as to British, Canadians and Americans. He had his special train parked in a

Planning D-Day: chiefs of the Allied Liberation Forces meet in London in February 1944. From front left – *Air Chief Marshal Sir Arthur Tedder, General Eisenhower, Montgomery;* (from back left) – *General Bradley, Admiral Ramsay, Air Chief Marshal Sir Trafford Leigh Mallory and General Bedell Smith.* (Imperial War Museum)

Montgomery visits a Glasgow munitions factory, April 1944. (Imperial War Museum)

siding near his headquarters, and toured the country, speaking not only to servicemen but to factory workers, dockers and railwaymen who would be helping to make and move the supplies 'his' armies would need. His message was clear: soldiers and civilians must get to know each other; they were in this war together.

Eventually, three million men would fight on the Allied side in Europe. Supplies for them were pouring in to Britain at the rate of a million tons a week. One convoy alone consisted of 42 ships bringing 1500 drive-off vehicles and another 2000 ready for assembly, plus 200 aircraft and 50,000 tons of general stores. The ships had to be offloaded and turned round in eight days, in order to make room for the next convoy. Seventy-five freight trains, with 10,000 wagons in tow, and countless lorries and trailers were needed to shift the input of this single convoy.

All the equipment had to be sorted and stored in

the reverse sequence to that in which it would be required for the front. Items needed to be painted with camouflage.

As D-Day approached, Britain became an armed camp. Even Sherwood Forest became an ammunition dump. The US Air Force needed 126 new airfields. The whole south-east coast from the Wash to Land's End was sealed off, and early in March strict controls were imposed on movements, telephone calls and mail. Shortly before D-Day, the men who were to take part in the historic landing were moved up from their concentration points in the rear to marshalling camps, where they were split up into groups linked with the ships in which they were to sail. In these camps, each man was briefed on his part in the operation. After that, no one was allowed to leave.

*   *   *

As usual, great efforts were made to deceive the Germans as to where the landings were to take place. As D-Day drew near, Montgomery moved his headquarters down to Southwick House, near Portsmouth. But his orders were sent by land telephone and broadcast from a transmitter in Kent, in order to give the impression that the invasion was to be mounted from somewhere near the Straits of Dover. For the same reason, the Royal Air Force was told that for each bomb that they dropped on targets in the Normandy area, they were to drop twice as many in the region around Calais. The deception worked so well that the German High Command kept some of their best Divisions in the Calais area, not only before the Allied landings but even after-wards. They thought it likely that the Normandy landings were only a feint.

The British Intelligence staff discovered an actor in Liverpool who was almost the double of Mont-gomery. Lieutenant Clifton James was serving in the Royal Army Pay Corps. He was trained to copy Montgomery's mannerisms – the set of his head, the way he walked with his hands clasped behind his back, the gestures he made with his hands, particu-larly when he disapproved of something, the habit he had of pinching his left cheek when deep in thought and so on. When James had learnt his part, he was flown to Gibraltar, and walked off the plane in daylight in full sight of German intelligence agents on the nearby Spanish frontier. On seeing 'Montgomery' they almost certainly concluded that more divisions would have to be kept in southern rather than in northern France.

There was much debate about the day on which the landings had best be made.

The Army would have preferred to carry out the assault by moonlight, if possible immediately after dusk, since this would give them the longest safe period during which their movements would be partially concealed from the enemy. But it would have to be a night when the moon would be giving enough light to see to clear mines. The Navy also favoured a night operation, which would help them to approach the Normandy coast undetected.

The landings themselves, however, would have to take place by daylight, so that the thousands of landing and assault craft could arrive correctly spaced and opposite the appointed landing places.

The bombers that were to protect the assault craft from enemy counter-attacks would also need daylight if they were to see their targets. So would the naval gunners who were to bombard the enemy from off-shore.

So it was decided that H-hour – the moment when the first assault craft would land – would need to be about an hour after the end of civil twilight: the moment at which the horizon can first be distinguished. Most of the approach would then be under cover of darkness.

The state of the tide was important, too. For some time, the Germans had been constructing obstacles known as 'hedgehogs' consisting of rows of steel spikes driven into the seabed. Some of them were designed to rip open the hulls of landing craft; others exploded a mine on contact. At various points, the rows of hedgehogs had been extended some way out to sea and were not visible until the tide was halfway out. Army 'sappers' would need half an hour to clear them away. So should the operation commence at low tide to allow the sappers the best conditions for their work? Perhaps; but then the troops would have to make their way across a large expanse of open beach, in the course of which they would be exposed to enemy fire. Clearly, the best plan would be to begin something like three hours before high water, on a rising tide. This would allow the sappers a fairly clear view of the hedgehogs while, at the same time, a rising tide would enable the 'returned empty' landing craft to make their way out to sea again without the risk of stranding.

So there were the conditions: a moonlit night, fol-

101

lowed by a day on which civil twilight would be due some three hours, but not more, before high water. These conditions would occur on only three days each month and, in June 1944, the three-day cycle began on June 5th. So June 5th was the date originally chosen for D-Day. By the end of March, the troops were already on the move towards the areas from which they would be shipped. All leave was stopped from April 6th. That month they practised landing exercises.

In the first week of April, all the general officers of Montgomery's armies were called together for a conference at which Churchill himself spoke. A large-scale assault rehearsal was carried out at the beginning of May.

On May 15th Eisenhower, as Supreme Commander, came to a presentation of Monty's invasion plans at St Paul's School. So did King George VI, Churchill and the British Chiefs of Staff. A week later, the King came down to Montgomery's headquarters outside Portsmouth to say goodbye. Finally, Montgomery made an eight-day tour in order to address all officers down to Lieutenant Colonel level, speaking to audiences of 500 to 600 at a time.

Then, when all the preparations had been made for a landing on June 5th, the weather broke.

Disturbing reports began to come in on June 3rd; there was a depression over the Azores out in the Atlantic. It was approaching Britain, and would probably sweep up the Channel on the night of June 4th/5th. Eisenhower therefore agreed to put off D-Day for 24 hours.

A meeting was arranged for 4 a.m. on June 5th.

As the commanders assembled, a near gale was still blowing up the Channel, but the weather reports suggested that it might have blown itself out by June 6th, and further, there might be a period of good weather for several days after June 6th.

There was still an element of chance, but a postponement till June 7th would have been disastrous in several ways. The smaller vessels would be perilously low on fuel and water by then. And, because high tide was later on that day, the landings could not have started until two hours after daylight. After that date, the next possible D-Day would have been nearly a fortnight away, or even a month, if the moon was taken into account – and during that time the troops, who already knew where they were to land, would have to spend some time ashore, with the risk the secrets of Overlord would leak out.

Eisenhower therefore decided that June 6th should be D-Day – though even he had his doubts, and prepared a notice that could be issued if the Allied landings failed and troops had to be recalled.

So there was just time to restart the operation as planned. Minesweepers cleared a path across the Channel through the enemy minefields. The Air Force attacked the enemy radar stations so successfully on the morning of D-Day that only one of them was left working – and the German commanders did not dare trust it.

The roads and railway lines along which enemy reinforcements would be sent had almost all been put out of action – except a few which were left open so large traffic blocks would build up on them, the perfect target for day bombers.

Never before in the history of warfare had there

Top and centre: *D-Day landings.* Below: *Montgomery and Bradley in a roadside conference, 24th June.* (Imperial War Museum)

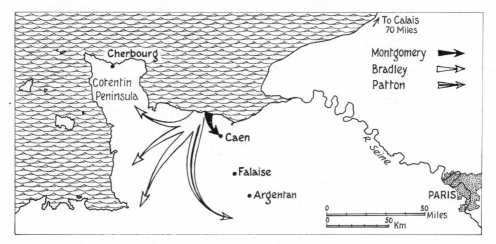

The Allied advance following the D-Day landings.

been such an armada. Some of the craft carried 'mattresses': mass-assemblies of rockets which could be fired as the vessels drew near the shore. Others had been loaded with anti-aircraft guns which could also be used before landing. Ahead of them went 'block-buster' vehicles designed to demolish the enemy 'hedgehogs'.

There were many types of tank. Some carried flails – chains which revolved in front of the tank and exploded mines before the tank reached them. Other tanks carried flame-throwers, and others again had fascines – rolls of brushwood which could be spread like a carpet over soft ground or craters. Some tanks were designed to be used as bridges which could help to get transport across defence ditches or small streams. Others could be used to help tanks surmount sea walls. Meanwhile, the Allies put more than 11,000 planes into the air; in the first 24 hours of Overlord they made 14,600 sorties.

By the night of June 7th, a quarter of a million men had been landed and, by D-Day plus four, a firm base 60 miles long and eight to twelve miles wide had been secured.

Only the Americans, on one of their landing beaches, had run into trouble. They were unlucky enough to meet a German force which was in the midst of a practice exercise aimed at repelling a possible Allied landing!

In most respects, the measures taken to mislead the German High Command had been particularly successful. Rommel, the Commander-in-Chief, had even left the front for a visit to Austria, believing that the weather was too bad for any attack.

*　　*　　*

Nevertheless, progress was slow – or so it seemed to those at home. The break-in to Normandy had gone well; the digging-in there had been a success, but people began to wonder when the break-out would come.

On June 19th the worst storm for forty years raged up the Channel and held up supplies for three vital days. Another difficulty was caused by the Germans, when they flooded a low-lying area of the country across which the Americans had hoped to advance. Elsewhere, on higher ground, the country was not suited to tanks; there were too many winding lanes, ditches and streams and high banks crowned with hedges. In short, it was good defensive country.

As Montgomery had foreseen, the real fighting took place around the city of Caen, to the south-east of the invasion peninsula. Roads and rail communications from both Paris and north-west France converged on Caen, and so, accordingly, did the German reinforcements. Montgomery reckoned that as these reinforcements arrived he would be able to draw them into an engagement from which they could not break off, and in which they would be destroyed piecemeal. And, indeed, this was what happened. More and more German troops were sent against the British to prevent the capture of Caen, while only a quarter of the enemy's tank force was directed against the Americans under General Bradley.

Yet Bradley made slow progress in sealing off the north of the Peninsula and capturing the vital port of Cherbourg. Cherbourg did not fall till June 24th and the rest of the peninsula remained unsealed for a further month.

During all this time, Montgomery appeared to be immobilised outside Caen.

But Caen was where Montgomery wanted to fight the Germans. There, and not after they had re-grouped further back on the far side of the Seine. Caen fell on July 10th, but even after this success Montgomery continued with his strategy of drawing the bulk of the German forces into the British and Canadian sector, and on July 27th Eisenhower's headquarters issued a depressing report saying that the Canadians had suffered a reverse (they had been driven back about 1000 yards during an advance movement).

The New York *Herald Tribune* came out with headlines ALLIES IN FRANCE BOGGED DOWN ON ENTIRE FRONT. At that moment, only Churchill and General Alan Brooke, Chief of the Imperial General Staff, stood by Montgomery.

Yet time was running out for the Germans, and, just when Eisenhower's headquarters were sending

An Allied convoy passes through Bayeux (Imperial War Museum)

out gloomy reports, Bradley's army, relieved by the
British and Canadians who had drawn off the bulk
of the German forces, was able to break through the
thin German crust of defence in his sector. Patton
was given a free hand to swing round towards Paris
behind the German line across open country and
with little opposition. By August 11th he had
reached Argentan and, still resentful towards Montgomery because of their quarrel in Sicily, he now
stirred up trouble by suggesting that he should be
allowed to go and brush the British aside from Caen
and into the sea 'like Dunkirk'.

108

It all looked as though the Americans had succeeded where Montgomery had failed. But Montgomery was more interested in defeating the enemy than in motoring across friendly country, and the Germans were now in danger of being cut off. They were crowded into a pocket from which they could escape to the east only through a narrow mouth. By August 13th, the US 12th Army had reached the southern corner of the mouth. Three days later, the Canadians reached the northern corner when they captured the key town of Falaise.

Before the week was out, the British and US forces joined together, and, though the gap was never closed in time to catch the entire German forces, the slaughter was immense. Twenty senior commanders were killed or captured. Two army commanders, one of them Rommel, had been wounded. (Rommel afterwards committed suicide.) About 40 enemy divisions had been destroyed or badly mauled; more than 1000 tanks had been destroyed, and the enemy had lost between 200,000 and 300,000 men.

It was Montgomery's finest victory. More impressive by far than El Alamein. The King approved his promotion to Field Marshal – the highest rank in the Army – with effect from September 1st.

Yet, that very day, the power of command was snatched away from him. Eisenhower announced that he was moving his headquarters from England to the Continent and was now assuming direct control of the Allied forces. From now on, Bradley would have equal status with Montgomery.

In some ways, this was the biggest setback in Montgomery's career.

11

Too Many Generals

Few people in Britain could understand why Montgomery should have been called on to give up overall command of the British, US and Canadian operations at the very moment when he had just won his most decisive victory. It looked like ingratitude, if not jealousy, on the part of his American allies.

True, the changeover by which Eisenhower was to take direct control of the whole front as soon as the battle for Normandy was over had been agreed by Winston Churchill well in advance of D-Day. Nevertheless, Montgomery saw the turn of events not merely as a misfortune for himself but as an obstacle to an early victory in Europe. He had shown them how to beat the Germans; so why couldn't they leave him to finish the job?

Montgomery's experience told him that the best strategy for achieving an early victory would be to strike a rapid and decisive blow at a critical point on the enemy's front – a single thrust up the coasts of Belgium and the Netherlands. The British and Canadian forces under his command were by themselves not capable of striking this blow at the moment when it would be most effective – immediately, while the German forces were still disorganised by the defeat they had just suffered. The thrust would have to be a combined operation with British,

Canadian and US troops under a single commander. He was even prepared to serve under General Bradley, if this were necessary, in order to establish a unified command. But Eisenhower would not agree. The British and American forces would, from then on, be split.

Eisenhower's view was that if a combined force was successful in advancing along the North Sea coast, as Montgomery wanted, it would be exposing a long flank to the enemy. Also, a large-scale attack could hardly be mounted until two major supply ports, Antwerp and Rotterdam, had both been captured and put to work again. And the Montgomery narrow front plan, by its nature, would leave some of the US forces marking time in the

Winter in the Netherlands, 1944/5 as British troops fight their way up the coastal strip. (Imperial War Museum)

south while all the action would take place in the north. Eisenhower preferred to attack everywhere, at all points, along a broad front.

Meanwhile, it was a grim struggle for the British and Canadians fighting their way on their own up the coastal strip. A long haul over flat, grey, featureless country crossed by dykes, canals and locks with each farm and each village looking like the last.

As predicted, Patton advanced in the south, was held up, ran out of supplies and called for more. The British were kept short, and partly as a result, failed in mid-September to secure a crucial bridge over the Lower Rhine at Arnhem – although Montgomery admitted to having made an error in not dropping parachutists closer to the bridge-head.

Then, in mid-December, the Germans launched a counter-offensive in the Ardennes area. They succeeded in taking the Allies by surprise. Bad weather and heavily wooded country made reconnaissance difficult, but, even so, a British intelligence source had warned General Bradley that some enemy movement had been detected and that this might mean an attack in his area. He is reported to have said 'Let them come'.

When they did, they chose the 100-mile area lying between the two main concentrations of General Bradley's 12th Army Group, moving among the trees through the grey dawn half-light. They found four US divisions: one was newly arrived, two were resting, and only one was battleworthy. Under the weight of the attack, the US communications broke down; it was hard to get a picture of what was happening. The centre of the US front was smashed open and 10,000 men of the US 106th Division sur-

A Daily Express *correspondent with airborne troops at Arnhem types his report.*
(Imperial War Museum)

rendered to a smaller force. For four days, Bradley
was out of touch with the situation in the north of
his command.

As the news worsened and the crisis deepened,
Eisenhower felt that only Montgomery could stop
the rot. On December 20th, he asked Montgomery to
take over from Bradley the control of two American
armies.

The measures which Montgomery took soon began
to slow the German advance. With two US armies
under his command, he was able to use the extra
strength to protect the most vital key points. Patton
was induced to wheel north to pinch out the German
'bulge'. By the middle of January, the main danger
was past. But Montgomery himself had a narrow
squeak.

The reason was that on December 29th Montgomery had written to Eisenhower pressing him to

113

appoint a single commander to control both
Bradley's 12th Army group and his own 21st Army
group.

To Montgomery this may have seemed a very
reasonable suggestion. To Eisenhower, however,
this seemed to be raising an issue that he thought
had been settled. The very thought of ordering
Bradley to serve under Montgomery – however well
it worked in a crisis – was unthinkable. Eisenhower
prepared a telegram telling Washington that either
Montgomery must go or he would have to. Freddie
de Guingand saw the telegram and persuaded
Eisenhower to hold it until Montgomery had been
warned. Only then did Montgomery back away from
the precipice; he told Eisenhower to tear up his
latest suggestions. In return, he gained something.
When the Battle of the Ardennes was safely over,
Montgomery was ordered to return one of the American armies to Bradley, but to keep the other.

*   *   *

By then, however, the War had little more than
three months to run, and, though the Russians were
first into Berlin and the Americans first across the
Rhine, it was to Montgomery that the Germans
made their first big surrender in the field.

At 11.30 on the morning of May 3rd, 1945 – the
day on which Hamburg fell to the Allies – four
senior German officers, led by General-Admiral von
Friedeburg, Commander-in-Chief of the German
Navy, were brought to Montgomery's Tactical Headquarters on Luneburg Heath, a sandy waste on
which manoeuvres are still carried out.

114

'Who are these men?' Montgomery barked when he saw them. His interpreter told him their names.

'What do they want?' It appeared that the officers wanted to arrange the surrender of three German armies who were being pressed towards Montgomery by the Russians.

'Can't accept,' Montgomery said brusquely. 'Not my front. Nothing to do with me. Not in my area. They must talk to the Russians.' Instead, he called on them to surrender all German armed forces on *his* front – in the Netherlands, north Germany, the North Sea islands, plus Denmark and the area to the south of it.

The officers said they could not do so. Taking them to his map room, Montgomery showed them the actual position on the front. They were very upset, and Montgomery felt sure they were ready to submit. He sent them away to lunch in a tent by themselves, with no one else except one staff officer present. One of the Germans broke down and wept; the others ate their meal almost in silence.

After lunch, Montgomery again asked them to surrender the forces in the areas concerned, without any 'ifs' or 'buts'. Otherwise the fighting would continue, and civilians as well as soldiers would be killed. (Privately, however, he had already given orders for offensive operations to cease; his troops had reached Lübeck, on the Baltic, ahead of the Red Army, thus saving Denmark from a Soviet occupation.)

The officers said that they could not surrender without authority from the Commander-in-Chief, Field Marshal Keitel.

Montgomery gave them until 6 o'clock the following evening to come to him with powers to sign a formal surrender.

War correspondents were called to watch the signing ceremony outside the caravan. It was as gloomy a scene as could be imagined – pouring with rain, and bitterly cold. Montgomery's caravan was parked against a sombre background of dark pine trees. Near to it was a tent in which stood an army wooden trestle table, covered with a grey army blanket. Round it were set six chairs.

Montgomery came down to the tent carrying in his hand the document he had prepared. The German officers saluted and took their seats. Montgomery read out the details. Hostilities on land, sea and air in the areas surrendered would cease at 8 o'clock British Double Summer Time the following morning, May 5th. The German Command would carry out at once, without argument or comment, all further orders issued by the Allied Powers on any subject. Disobedience would be treated as a breach of the surrender terms. The surrender document was typed out in English; there were German copies but the English text was the authentic one, and the decision of the Allied Powers would be final if any doubt or dispute arose as to the meaning or interpretation of the surrender terms.

Then Montgomery ordered the Germans to sign the document. When the last German name had been added, he signed himself on behalf of Eisenhower. 'And that concludes the surrender,' he said, getting up from his chair.

This was the moment to which six years of struggle had led – across the sands of the desert, through the mud of Italy and the din of Normandy

Montgomery reads the terms of surrender to the German delegation, 4th May 1945. General-Admiral Von Friedeburg is sitting on his right. Inset: The Instrument of Surrender: Montgomery sent Eisenhower a photostat and refused to part with the original. (Imperial War Museum)

and the ice and snow of the Ardennes. Montgomery took the document and sent photostats of it to Eisenhower. He refused during his lifetime to part with the original.

A general surrender over the rest of the front followed on May 7th.

The war in Europe was over at last.

12

Life at the Top

But was the War really over? Apparently not. For, although Hitler's armed forces had been defeated, there was no German government that the victors were prepared to recognise. The four main allies, Britain, France, the United States and the Soviet Union, formed a Control Commission of four members, one from each ally, to rule the country as a whole; and the land was divided into four Occupation Zones, one for each ally. After some delay Montgomery was named as Controller of the British Zone, which covered the north-west of the country, and as British representative in the Control Commission.

Meanwhile, he began, at first entirely on his own responsibility, to look after the welfare of twenty million Germans in his area. There were more than a million German prisoners who had to be fed and guarded, and another million wounded who needed medical care. The shortage of food and the weakened resistance of the people raised the risks of epidemics which could spread with terrifying speed.

Montgomery's solution was to hold the prisoners in peninsulas along the coastline, with their backs to the sea. They were to be released and sent out in civilian clothes as soon as there was work for them. Farm workers were urgently needed to get in the harvest. So were mine workers, who could provide fuel for the coming winter, and seamen, who could restart the fishing industry. No Allied troops were allowed to use German cars or lorries without special permission. The vehicles would be needed to move and feed Germans. The troops were also forbidden to buy food in German shops. Montgomery knew that every ounce would be required by the Germans themselves. He also banned Service wives from joining their husbands; they, too, would be a drain on German resources.

Montgomery also hastened to put the country on its feet by restarting its factories. He reckoned that if he failed to do so, the whole cost of the occupation

German prisoners at Lübeck, taken when the 11th Armoured Division captured the town, on 3rd May 1945. (Imperial War Museum)

would fall on the British taxpayer. Also, if there was no improvement in their living conditions, the Germans would begin to despair of the future, and might even long for the return of the good old days under Hitler – or perhaps turn to Communism.

The Russians, perhaps for this very reason, took the opposite view. They stripped the machinery from the factories in their zone and sent it back to the Soviet Union. Unlike the British and Americans, they did not bring their own food with them but 'lived off the land', that is, off the Germans, and the people faced starvation. Many were compelled to flee to the West, adding to the food problems in the British, American and French zones. The Russian policy of bankrupting their own zone made it impossible to run the country as a single economic unit, and, in the end, the three Western powers decided to manage the economy of their areas independently.

The Russians also prevented the four-power Control Commission, which was supposed to rule Germany as a whole, from getting down to work. The Western Allies found that they were not welcome in the Soviet Zone.

All this gave Montgomery plenty of work. The Germans were not the only people he had to look after. He had to keep in touch with other Zone Controllers and with his own troops, to 'keep them in the picture'. Boredom would be fatal for them and for their relations with the German population.

One day, towards the end of August, while flying to visit a Canadian unit, Montgomery's plane crashed. The pilot escaped unhurt and so did Montgomery's aide, but the aircraft was a write-off and Montgomery was badly shaken and had to break off in the middle of his speech to the Canadians. He flew back unconcernedly, but his spine was injured and this led to lung trouble and attacks of arthritis.

But at least, in the British Zone, the population got through the winter without disaster, and the reins of government were gradually being transferred from the military to the German civilians.

*　　*　　*

Meanwhile Montgomery continued to gather honours around him. He had received the Order of Victory from the Russian leader, Stalin, and similar decorations came from the American, French, Belgian, Dutch, Danish, Polish, Greek, Moroccan, Tunisian and other governments. He received the freedom of seventeen British cities, and honorary degrees from half a dozen universities.

In the New Year's Honours List he was raised to the peerage and became Viscount Montgomery of Alamein. Later in January he was told that he had been selected for the appointment of Chief of the Imperial General Staff, the highest professional post in the British Army.

Once again, Montgomery's promotion had not been a foregone conclusion. The Labour Government was still obsessed with fears that he might turn out to be a military dictator. Politicians were afraid that he would upset too many people – including themselves; and know-alls predicted that he would turn up at the War Office wearing a funny hat and would start sacking everyone. (He did arrive wearing his usual beret.)

Once home, Montgomery found that the Government of the day, like the one a quarter of a century earlier, had little time for the armed forces. It was more interested in nationalising private industry, launching the Welfare State, and in raising the school leaving age. So Montgomery's first trip abroad after taking over his new job was hardly likely to please the Cabinet. He went to Canada and the United States, where he proceeded to hold a conference with Eisenhower and other military leaders on how World War III ought to be fought. He had always said that he was a simple soldier and unversed in politics, but one could never be certain that he was being serious.

Politicians were not sure which they disliked most, Montgomery's visits abroad – when he discussed delicate questions such as the possibility of withdrawing British troops from Egypt, India or Greece, or had talks with Stalin (when the Ambassador from the Foreign Office had no such luck) – or his months at home, when he campaigned for longer compulsory military service, better pay and conditions for the Services, and more money for weapons.

He frequently bypassed the War Office and went direct to Clement Attlee, who had succeeded Winston Churchill as Prime Minister, and at one time plotted to get Attlee's Defence Minister of the day replaced by someone who would suit him (Montgomery) better.

Then, in 1948, relief came for the Government. Montgomery was offered, and accepted, a top job in Europe – in the organisation that afterwards developed into the North Atlantic Treaty Organisation, the body that unites the defence forces of Britain, Canada, the United States, West Germany,

Italy and other western European powers. He served for ten years as NATO's Deputy Supreme Commander – training, inspecting and invigorating the alliance, though he never ceased to be appalled by the long-winded, indecisive and purposeless discussion papers that often came his way.

*   *   *

Then he retired, although, as a Field Marshal, he remained permanently on the active list.

Even after retiring, Montgomery went on travelling. He visited China, Central America, South Africa and Egypt, where his talk with Colonel Nasser, the Egyptian leader, once more troubled the Foreign Office.

He wrote his *Memoirs* and several books on his campaigns. He enjoyed broadcasting, and his words, spoken crisply and clearly, came across well. He was heard on the *Desert Island Discs* programme, and, when asked which book he would most like to take with him to his desert island, he chose his own *History of Warfare*.

His views were often in advance of their day. As far back as 1965, he warned the United States that they must withdraw from south-east Asia and would have to recognise Communist China. He was also one of the earliest to favour 'brighter cricket'.

He was a keen supporter of the Portsmouth Football Club, but shook his head over the decline, as he saw it, in the standards of skiing. Skiers of the 'fifties, relied too much on ski-hoists, he believed, and would not know how to cope with overland trekking in wet snow.

Soon after the end of the War, Montgomery had set up a home for himself in the Hampshire country-side in an old mill at Isington on the River Wey.

As he grew older, Montgomery became more and more attached to his home.

Those who went to visit the Field Marshal noticed that, though he ate only the plainest food himself, his guests did extremely well, and enjoyed themselves. He was a good host, and went to considerable trouble to see that the wines were good – though he drank none himself. Even his undoubted vanity could be endearing. Asked to name the three greatest commanders in history, he said, 'The other two were Alexander the Great and Napoleon,' and it was almost impossible to tell whether he was joking.

Towards friends he was loyal – in particular towards Winston Churchill, whom he visited not only when he was in power, but also when he was ill and dispirited. Churchill's delight was to see the irrepressible Montgomery outmanoeuvred at croquet.

Towards his own family he was less forthcoming. There was a memorable occasion when Montgomery refused to allow his mother to be invited to a ceremonial lunch at which he was to be made an honorary freeman of the city of Newport. To the end, he was jealous of anyone who, he felt, was trying to bask in his reflected glory – even of Freddie de Guingand, who had served him so well as Chief of Staff. He did not choose de Guingand as Vice Chief of the Imperial General Staff – though, to be fair to Montgomery, it must be said that he felt it was not in the Army's best interests for all the top jobs to go to 'Montgomery men'.

He was most at home with young people. 'I have always been a great believer in youth, with its enthusiasm, optimism, originality, and willingness to follow a leader,' he once said. He supported both the National Association of Boys' Clubs and the Outward Bound Trust. He was always pleased when young people came to visit him – and kept an enormous cask of peanut butter, which he knew was popular with them.

The Field Marshal in retirement, with his grandchildren Arabella and Henry, at Isington. (Col. Brian Montgomery) Inset: *The garden at Isington Mill.* (Imperial War Museum)

Today, Montgomery's body lies beneath a yew tree close to the church at Binsted in Hampshire, where he had worshipped for twenty-five years. His caravans have moved on from the barns at Isington to their place in the Imperial War Museum. Earlier, a gigantic motor cycle stood with them, presented to Montgomery after he had opened some industrial exhibition. 'Field Marshal,' asked a small boy who had come with friends on a visit, 'When you die what will you do with it?'

Montgomery smiled. 'I won't care then,' he said.

Acknowledgments

I am grateful for the permission given to me to quote three passages from Field Marshal Montgomery's *Forward to Victory*, published by Hutchinson, and two passages from his *Memoirs*, published by Collins.

I should also like to thank the present Viscount Montgomery for his help during the preparation of the final chapter and Colonel Brian Montgomery, the Field Marshal's brother, for his generosity in lending family photographs.

Unless credited to Colonel Montgomery or other sources, the photographs in this book come from the Imperial War Museum, whose very helpful and efficient staff I should also like to thank.

J.O.H.F.

Index

Index